SAUCE
by Ciara Elizabeth Smyth

SAUCE was first performed at Bewley's Café Theatre, Dublin, as part of Dublin Fringe Festival on 10 September 2019. It was revived at Bewley's on 10 January 2022.

CAST

MAURA   Camille Lucy Ross
MELLA   Clodagh Mooney Duggan

CREATIVE TEAM

Director   Jeda de Brí
Set & Costume Designer   Ellen Kirk
Sound Designer   Jennifer O'Malley
Lighting Designer   Colm Maher
Choreographer   Jade O'Connor
Stage Manager   Ciara Nolan

INTRODUCTION
Ciara Elizabeth Smyth

If you are reading this, I presume you are either interested in theatre or you are my mother and father. In the case of the latter, hello parents, lovely to have you here. Can you make stew next time I'm home?

In the case of the former, if you are thinking about making theatre, please do. Disregard any misgivings, worries or insecurities. We all have them and we do it anyway. As one of my favourite writers once said: 'Theatre is the warmest and most democratic of art forms. It requires only other people to do it and there are lots of them, everywhere.'

SAUCE and *All honey* are very different plays (despite both containing, frankly, too many references to condiments), but I think they're essentially trying to do the same thing, which is to find humour in pain. Instead of explaining these plays any further, and since theatre is a collaborative medium that needs only people, I will do something far more important and mention the people behind them.

Neither *SAUCE* nor *All honey* would have seen the light of day without the spectacular people at Dublin Fringe Festival and the Irish Theatre Institute. I am one of the many who has benefited, and continues to benefit, from their generosity, expertise and tenacity. For that, I am tremendously grateful.

I have also been helped immeasurably by Fishamble: The New Play Company, who had a hand in both plays. Their endless support, kindness and encouragement not only gave me the means but the confidence to keep writing.

David Horan, Iseult Golden and Colm Maher at Bewley's Café Theatre *are* national treasures. They approached me about remounting both plays directly after their Fringe runs and they have stuck with *SAUCE* for almost two years. (*SAUCE* was due to be revived in March 2020, but something happened that year, I can't remember what, and it was cancelled.) Nick Hern Books have also been unwavering in its support.

Jeda de Brí, who directed both plays and is essentially a magician, poured her genius into the productions and deserves any and all praise for their successes. I am indebted to Oisín Kearney, for his advice, humour and the most helpful feedback I have ever received. I would be lost without him. And I am eternally grateful to all the actors and creatives who have been involved with these plays, from workshops to stage; they made everything better.

And finally, the actor and creator Camille Lucy Ross has been (and remains) the most important and inspiring artist to me. Her talent, energy and sensitivity is unparalleled.

To her, I dedicate *SAUCE* and I look forward to years of laughing, messing, playing, failing and winning with her.

I hope you enjoy these plays as much as I've enjoyed working with the people behind them.

BIOGRAPHIES

Camille Lucy Ross (*Maura*)
Camille is a graduate of Ecole Philippe Gaulier, LA's iO West Improv
School, The Gaiety School of Acting, and University College Dublin.
She most recently appeared in *Callan's Kicks* (RTÉ) and is a series
regular. Camille is also a writer, improviser and founder of Brazen
Tales Productions for which she wrote and performed in *Big Bobby*.
Little Bobby (First Fortnight Winner) and *How To be Angry* (Best
Ensemble nominee). Theatre credits include *The Treaty* (Fishamble),
The Fall of the Second Republic (Corn Exchange), *The Odd Couple* (The
Everyman), *We Can't Have Monkeys in the House* (New Theatre). Other
TV and film credits include *The Rafters* (John Carney/Warehouse),
Finding Joy (Treasure) *Republic of Telly* and *Bridget & Eamon* (RTÉ).

Clodagh Mooney Duggan (*Mella*)
Clodagh's most recent theatre credits include *Eleanora Salter and the
Monster from the Sea* and *Dogs of War* by Fionn Foley. Other theatre
credits include *All honey* by Ciara Elizabeth Smyth, *A Day in May*
directed by Gerard Stembridge (Olympia and national tour), *Tryst*
(national tour and VAULT Festival), *Susie and The Story Shedder*
(national tour), *King Lear* (The Mill Theatre), *The Snow Queen* (Smock
Alley), Second Age's *Hamlet* (Helix) and *Cirque de Rêves* (Smock Alley
and Bewley's Café Theatre). Her film and TV credits include *Dub Daze*,
Cumann Na Bman (TG4), and most recently *Red Election*.

Ciara Elizabeth Smyth (*Playwright*)
Ciara Elizabeth Smyth is an award-winning writer for stage and
screen. Her plays have been presented by the Abbey Theatre,
Fishamble, Dublin Fringe, the MAC Theatre, Project Arts Centre and
Bewley's Café Theatre. Currently, Ciara is on commission to adapt her
debut play *All honey* (Fishamble New Writing Award 2017) and her
2019 play *SAUCE* for television, with Buccaneer Media and Maia
Pictures, respectively. She is also on commission with Chapter One
Pictures for a television project and is being supported by
Summerhall, Edinburgh, and mentored by Enda Walsh to write a new
play. She was a recipient of the Next Generation Award 2020, the
Lyric Theatre's Live to Digital Commission 2021 and the Abbey
Theatre's Commemoration Bursary 2021. Ciara is represented by
Curtis Brown.

Jeda de Brí (*Director*)
Jeda de Brí is an award-winning director and writer for stage and screen. She has directed work for the Abbey Theatre and Fishamble, as well as writing and directing new plays at Project Arts Centre, VAULT Festival in London and the Lyric Theatre Belfast. She is currently developing feature films with Screen Ireland, Samson Films and Treasure Entertainment.

Ellen Kirk (*Set & Costume Designer*)
Ellen is a Dublin-based designer for stage and screen. Recent stage design credits include costume design for *Straight to Video* by Emmet Kirwan, directed by Phillip McMahon (Landmark Productions, Civic Theatre and Project Arts Centre, 2021); set design for *Masterclass* by Brokentalkers and Adrienne Truscott (Project Arts Centre, Dublin Fringe Festival, 2021), and *On A House Like A Fire* by Michelle Read and Brian Keegan (Smock Alley, Bealtaine Festival, 2021). Recent film production design credits include *An Encounter* by Mark O'Halloran, directed by Kelly Campbell (winner of Academy Award-qualifying Grand Prix Irish Short at Cork International Film Festival, 2021) and *Don't Go Where I Can't Find You* by Rioghnach Ní Ghrioghair and Samson Films. Ellen has worked with numerous music artists on stage designs, live visuals, photoshoots and music videos including Kojaque, Soft Boy Records and Soda Blonde. www.ellenkirkdesign.com

Jennifer O'Malley (*Sound Designer*)
Jennifer is a composer and sound designer based in Dublin who is a classically trained multi-instrumentalist and vocalist. She has worked as a session cellist in the past, and currently scores music and sound for film and theatre. Some of her theatre credits include *Summertime* (Dublin Fringe, 2018, Drogheda Arts Festival, 2019, Abbey Young Curators Festival, 2019, as sound designer and composer), *SAUCE* (Bewley's Café Theatre, 2019), *Beckett's Room* (The Gate, 2019, as assistant sound designer), *Restoration* (Project Arts Centre, 2020), *Will I See You There* (Dublin Fringe, 2020, as sound designer), *Before You Say Anything* (Dublin Fringe, 2020, as composer), *Ar Ais Arís* (Brightening Air, 2021, as sound designer), *Where Sat the Lovers* (Dublin Fringe, 2021, as composer and sound designer with Leon Henry), *Masterclass* (Dublin Fringe, 2021, as composer and sound designer). www.jenny.ie

Jade O'Connor (*Choreographer*)
Jade is a multidisciplinary performer and theatremaker whose work includes dance theatre, TV, film, theatre, visual art and music. After graduating on a scholarship from Millennium Performing Arts, London, she began working and collaborating with various directors, artists and theatre companies. Jade is an award-winning performer and creator. She has performed both nationally and internationally at festivals and stages from the Ramallah Contemporary Dance Festival in Palestine to Dublin Fringe and Dublin Dance Festival and from The National Theatre of Jerusalem to our own National Theatre, the Abbey. Most notably she has worked with Broken Talkers, Catherine Young Dance Theatre, THISISPOPBABY, Sibéal Davitt Dance and Fidget Feet.

Colm Maher (*Lighting Designer*)
Colm is the technical and front-of-house manager of Bewley's Café Theatre. He has designed lighting for most of the theatre's in-house productions and many touring productions. He is production manager for Bewley's Café Theatre in Dublin Fringe Festival every year and has overseen and lit most of the Fishamble/Irish Theatre Institute's Show-in-a-Bag and Duets programme. Other lighting design work includes *Tuesday's with Morrie* at the Gaiety Theatre, Dublin, and the Lyric Theatre Belfast, and Connected at Project Upstairs. In 2021 he was the creator and producer of Bewley's Café Theatre's inaugural *WALKABOUT* season, a series of outdoor performances set in Dublin's historic parks.

Ciara Nolan (*Stage Manager*)
Ciara has been a freelance stage manager for many years and is a graduate of The Lir Academy. Ciara is delighted to be back working on *SAUCE* at Bewley's for a second time after the Dublin Fringe Festival in 2019. Some of Ciara's recent theatre credits are Jack Thorne's *Mydidae*, Brendan Behan's *Borstal Boy*, *Wicked*, *Shrek The Musical* and the Gaiety pantos.

BEWLEY'S CAFÉ THEATRE

Artistic Director	David Horan
Producer/Administrator	Iseult Golden
FOH/Technical Manager	Colm Maher

Bewley's Café Theatre is proud to be a home for new writing in Irish Theatre. Situated on the second floor of Dublin's legendary Grafton Street Café, since opening its doors in 1999 the Café Theatre has emerged as Ireland's foremost venue for Lunchtime Drama, presenting classic and (almost) forgotten one-act plays alongside contemporary Irish and international work.

The Café Theatre has garnered a reputation for innovation and excellence while maintaining a uniquely Irish and personal touch. Our vision is to be a vital cog in the creation and revival of great plays and to be a springboard for artists to wider audiences. Bewley's Café Theatre aims to stage the best stories from emerging, mid-career and established artists, stretching the boundaries of what can be achieved in an hour of theatre.

Praise for Bewley's Café Theatre

'A very special venue… Bewley's Café Theatre is a national treasure.' *Irish Independent*
'Bewley's Café Theatre goes from strength to strength.' *Irish Times*
'Bewley's lunchtime theatre has become a revered institution.' *Irish Theatre Magazine*
'I felt my soul was nourished at lunchtime.' *The View*, RTÉ 1
'One of Dublin's hidden treasures.' RTÉ, Radio 1

www.bewleyscafetheatre.com

SAUCE

For Camille

SAUCE was first performed at Bewley's Café Theatre, Dublin, as part of Dublin Fringe Festival, on 10 September 2019, with the following cast and creative team:

MAURA	Camille Lucy Ross
MELLA	Ciara Elizabeth Smyth

Director	Jeda de Brí
Producer	Donnacha O'Dea
Set & Costume Designer	Ellen Kirk
Sound Designer	Jennifer O'Malley
Lighting Designer	Colm Maher
Choreographer	Jade O'Connor
Stage Manager	Ciara Nolan
Photography & Graphics	Ste Murray

It was revived at Bewley's on 10 January 2022, with the following cast and creative team:

MAURA	Camille Lucy Ross
MELLA	Clodagh Mooney Duggan

Director	Jeda de Brí
Set & Costume Designer	Ellen Kirk
Sound Designer	Jennifer O'Malley
Lighting Designer	Colm Maher
Choreographer	Jade O'Connor
Stage Manager	Ciara Nolan

SAUCE was supported by DUETS, an artist development initiative of Dublin Fringe Festival, Fishamble: The New Play Company and Irish Theatre Institute.

Characters

MAURA

Also plays:
PADDY
LORRAINE
HEALY
FAT WATCH LEADER A
BITCH B
FATHER DESMOND

MELLA

Also plays:
PHILIP
GHOST OF DOLLY PARTON
FAT WATCH LEADER B
BITCH A
SIOBHAN
THE HUMMER MOONEY

Note on Text

This is a multi-locational, multi-roling play. The characters and various locations should be created by the physicality of the actors without the need for additional props and costume.

A dash (–) denotes an interruption by action.

A forward slash (/) denotes overlapping speech or an interruption by another character speaking.

An ellipsis (…) denotes a character trailing off or struggling to find the end of the sentence.

This text went to press before the end of rehearsals and so may differ slightly from the play as performed.

Taster

Music swells – (Ref. Mango – 'Bad Man'). Actors enter dancing.

Music and movement cuts simultaneously.

MAURA. Sweet and sour.

MELLA. Piri-piri.

MAURA. Black bean.

MELLA. Kung Pao.

MAURA. Sweet chili.

MELLA. Mayonnaise.

MAURA. Ketchup.

MELLA. Curry.

MAURA. Garlic.

MELLA. Gravy.

MAURA. Taco.

MELLA. Salsa.

MAURA. Soy.

   Brief pause.

MELLA. There is no better feeling /

MAURA. Than ordering a takeaway.

MELLA. Better even than the eating /

MAURA. Is the ordering.

MELLA. And better even than the food /

MAURA. Is the sauce.

MELLA. It enhances flavour.

MAURA. From bland to bliss.

MELLA. So all I can think about.

MAURA. All I want to think about.

MELLA. Right now.

MAURA. Is sauce.

Brief pause.

Online is quicker.

MELLA. I call to order.

MAURA. Pick a freckle on my arm.

MELLA. Check the time while I wait.

MAURA. Where is the food?

MELLA. Where the fuck is the food?

MAURA. Because now that it's ordered.

MELLA. But not yet delivered.

MAURA. I have time to think.

MELLA. And I don't want time to think.

MAURA. I don't want to think about – Doorbell!

MELLA. Thank fuck.

MAURA. Hereyougocheersthanksbye.

MELLA. Hi, hey. How are you? Hope you don't mind the change. Yeah, yeah it's still money yeah, gas. Hey listen, oh he's gone.

MAURA. I go to the kitchen, get a fork.

MELLA. I sit on the floor of the hall.

MAURA. And begin.

MELLA. I don't stop.

MAURA. There's sauce on my face.

MELLA. Smudged on my chin.

MAURA. Dripping down my neck.

MELLA. On my cheeks.

MAURA. In my eyebrows.

MELLA. My hair.

MAURA. My elbows.

MELLA. I indulge.

MAURA. I engorge.

MELLA. I allow myself to be free.

MAURA. Before I realise.

MELLA. The food is gone.

MAURA. And I'm still standing at the drawer.

MELLA. Still sitting on the floor.

MAURA. When I remember why I'm sleeping in the stockroom at work.

MELLA. The reason I'm alone in my family home.

MAURA. Close my eyes, try to forget.

MELLA. What happened earlier.

MAURA. But I can't.

TOGETHER. Get. Rid.

One

MELLA. Sharp and sour South Dublin suburb. Newsagent's.
  Chipper. Church. Chemist's. Pub. Pub. Pub. Pub. Pub. GAA[1]
  club. All sons on the rugby team, daughters on the hockey
  team. Debate captains, golf societies, boutique flower shops
  and gourmet-food delicatessens, the place can't move for
  the money.

None of which I have.

Into the apartment I share with my nanny and /

PADDY. SURPRISE!

MELLA. Jesus fuck.

PADDY. Did I get you?

MELLA. Christ, Paddy. (*To the audience*.) Nanny's brother,
  Paddy.

PADDY. I got you.

MELLA. Why did you do that?

PADDY. Listen, I have some bad news.

MELLA. What?

PADDY. Bad news. I've been trying to call you.

MELLA. I was busy doing good deeds. (*To the audience*.) I was
  watching porn on my phone in a park.

PADDY. No you weren't, you little liar.

MELLA. I was. Great deeds.

PADDY. You should have answered.

MELLA. Why?

PADDY. Because your grandmother passed away this morning.

  Silence.

MELLA (*in disbelief*). Fuck off.

1. Pronounced GAH

PADDY. Yeah. (*Pause. Brightly.*) Okay bye.

MELLA. Wait what?

PADDY. I have to leg it.

MELLA. She's dead?

PADDY. She is. Tragic. (*Brief pause.*) See ya.

MELLA. Paddy. What happened?

PADDY. Ugh. The panic alarm was pressed and the company called me.

MELLA. How did she /

PADDY. Heart problem. Runs in the family. (*Registers her shock.*) Please don't get emotional, I really can't stay.

MELLA. Why?

PADDY. I just. (*Sighs.*) I don't want to.

MELLA. Why did they call you?

PADDY. I was her emergency contact.

MELLA. Oh.

PADDY. Plus I was in the St John's Ambulance so I'm fully trained for medical situations.

MELLA. Are you drunk?

PADDY. Not yet. But it's Friday somewhere.

MELLA. It's Friday here.

PADDY. Brilliant. I'll be in the pub, so.

MELLA. Where is she?

PADDY. St James' morgue presumably.

MELLA. Do I have to go to the morgue?

PADDY. I don't know death etiquette.

MELLA. Paddy, what do we do?

PADDY. I'm going to the pub. Maybe you should start packing?

MELLA. I don't want to pack up her things.

PADDY. No. (*Beat.*) Look I'd really rather do this over text.

MELLA. Do what over text?

PADDY. It's not your apartment. So pack your things.

MELLA. But I live here.

PADDY. Yeah but. It's actually not yours. Is it?

MELLA. No it's my nanny's.

PADDY. It was. Now it's mine.

MELLA. How?

PADDY. I'll get it. In the will.

MELLA. She didn't have a will.

PADDY. She did have a will.

MELLA. She didn't have a will.

PADDY. Oh she had a will.

MELLA. Why would you get it? You do nothing for her.

PADDY. Did.

MELLA. Did, Jesus.

PADDY. I was her only brother. And she has no children now.

MELLA. But I was her carer and her only grandchild.

PADDY. Yes. But she always said you were a filthy liar and she wouldn't piss on you if you were on /

MELLA. Okay yes thank you.

PADDY. You're welcome.

MELLA. Well, that's fine, Paddy, because I actually don't want the apartment – (*To the audience.*) I do want the apartment.

PADDY. Great. See how easy everything is when you tell the truth.

MELLA. Yeah.

PADDY. You can go live with your parents.

MELLA. They're dead, Paddy.

PADDY. Still dead, are they?

MELLA. Yes.

PADDY. Listen, Mella. I seriously have to go, this conversation is very, very boring to me.

MELLA. I'd like to see the will, in case she left me anything.

PADDY. Really?

MELLA. Yes.

PADDY. Ugh. Well, I don't have the will.

MELLA. No problem, I'll go see her solicitor. Today.

PADDY. Fine. Sorted. Bye now, love.

PADDY *leaves*.

MELLA. Hi, can I order for delivery please?

Two

Earlier than Taster and One.

MAURA (*to the audience*). Sweet and salty South Dublin suburb. Newsagent's. Pub. Chipper. Pub. Church. Pub. Chemist's. Pub. GAA club. (*Counts*.) Pub. Ladies who lunch, wine-and-book club. Husbands who golf, drink, and laugh. Chinese-food takeaway up the top and train station down the bottom of the most suffocating peninsula in the entire county.

Midnight, I wake up in the bed I share with my husband and –

PHILIP *is having sex with* LORRAINE.

PHILIP. Oh, Lorraine.

LORRAINE. Oh, Philip. Ride me like a road instructor.

PHILIP. What?

LORRAINE. Driving instructor, driving instructor. Just do me.

PHILIP. Okay. Oh, Lorraine.

MAURA (*to the audience*). Light on. Husband in bed with me, staring at me. Naked and not alone. On top of a vaguely familiar blonde mop, thrusting violently. He's fucking someone else in the bed beside me.

LORRAINE. Jesus, stop there's a woman in the bed!

PHILIP. I'm almost finished.

MAURA (*to the woman*). He needs to finish.

PHILIP. AH. Finished.

PHILIP *catches his breath.*

LORRAINE. Who the fuck is in the bed?

MAURA. It's me. His wife.

PHILIP. My wife.

LORRAINE. His what? His wife? You have a wife? Jesus Christ. I'm out. Delete those pictures of my tits.

PHILIP. Close over that door on your way. Thanks, Michelle.

LORRAINE. Lorraine.

PHILIP. That's the one.

Silence.

Now. I think that makes us even.

MAURA. What?

PHILIP. Even, love. Quitsies.

MAURA. Why did you do that?

PHILIP. You hurt me, so I hurt you.

MAURA. I can't believe you just did that.

PHILIP. Don't shout at me, Maura. You're a disgrace. You stole a jumper from a charity shop.

MAURA. I know but /

PHILIP. I am vice president of the lacrosse club, Maura. Did you even think about lacrosse? If the boys found out you were in a charity shop…

MAURA. I said I was sorry.

PHILIP. This isn't the first time either, is it?

MAURA. No.

PHILIP. No, we know all about your sticky fingers. Jewellery, greeting cards, loose sauce packets from fast-food emporiums. Fast food, Maura. Sauce. You know sauce / makes you fat.

MAURA. Makes me fat, yes I know.

PHILIP. That Guard that brought you home, Diarmuid. He is a close personal friend. I have to play racquetball with him tomorrow.

MAURA. I didn't know that.

PHILIP. How am I supposed to show my face at the pre-racquetball continental breakfast buffet, Maura? Did you even think about that?

MAURA. I genuinely didn't.

PHILIP. Well, this is it for me. Things are going to change.

MAURA. In what way?

PHILIP. Starting tomorrow. You're going on a diet. You've gotten fat like a whale and I can't get hard with you. Captain Healy is soft. Hence Michelle.

MAURA. Lorraine.

PHILIP. That's the one. And you're quitting your job in the newsagent's. It's done you no good being around all those sweets and things to steal.

MAURA. But /

PHILIP. But what?

MAURA. I don't want to quit my job.

PHILIP. Because you'll miss all your friends? You have no friends.

MAURA. I don't see how that's relevant.

PHILIP. We're not having this discussion.

MAURA. You just had sex with someone else.

PHILIP. That was your fault.

MAURA. How?

PHILIP. For the reasons I just said.

MAURA. I don't want to quit my job.

PHILIP. Tell you what, Maura. If you love that job so much why don't you just marry it?

MAURA. What?

PHILIP. Marry your job. See if it pays the bills and gives you pocket money.

MAURA. It does give me money.

PHILIP. Well, then go to your 'job'.

MAURA. But I don't start work for another ten hours.

PHILIP. Go early today. Yeah, why don't you do that? Why don't you sleep in the shop tonight? Go and think about what you did.

MAURA. What I did?

PHILIP. Just go.

MAURA. Okay. Fine.

MAURA *leaves*.

Pause.

Chinese food meal takeaway after midnight delivery South Dublin. Search.

Three

Later than One.

MELLA. Belly full of food and bouncing, I am bulling. I am not a child. I do not need my uncle's permission to live in my dead grandmother's apartment. I have rights. I'm almost sure of it. I am not about to up and leave my home just because she is dead. Pack my bags? Pack *my* bags? We will see who's packing whose bags soon. Solicitor's office, hold the buzzer, ready my phone voice and /

HEALY. Ms Donnelly, I am so sorry for your loss.

MELLA (*to the audience*). Solicitor. Healy. Oily fella. (*To* HEALY.) I need to see my nanny's will.

HEALY. Whoa, easy, girl. Step into my office. How are you feeling?

MELLA. Fine.

HEALY. What did the hospital say?

MELLA. She's dead.

HEALY. Tragic.

MELLA. Yeah.

HEALY. Okay, small talk over.

MELLA. Can I see it please, Mr Healy?

HEALY. Mella, call me Phil.

MELLA. Okay yeah great I will. The apartment?

HEALY. Yes, your grandmother's apartment /

MELLA. Is now my apartment?

HEALY. Not exactly.

MELLA. Not exactly?

HEALY. She's left it to your Uncle Paddy.

MELLA (*to the audience*). Fuck.

HEALY. Hmmm?

MELLA. Really? Did she leave any money?

HEALY. She didn't.

MELLA. Where did her savings go?

HEALY. You didn't know?

MELLA. Didn't know what?

HEALY. She was an alcoholic.

MELLA. Oh no I knew that, everyone knew that.

HEALY. Okay good. Your uncle told me he'd like to sell the apartment asap.

MELLA (*to the audience*). Bastard. (*To* HEALY.) You've seen him already?

HEALY. He called.

MELLA. I see. Did she leave me anything?

HEALY. She did actually, let's see. Ah, here we go, Specific Bequests.

MELLA (*to the audience*). Please be diamonds.

HEALY. I leave to Mella Donnelly, of Dún Chaoin, Co. Dublin, Republic of Ireland, if they shall survive me, for their own use absolutely, the following: Charm Bracelet.

MELLA. Charm bracelet?

HEALY. Charm bracelet.

MELLA (*to the audience*). Charm bracelet as in the only piece of jewellery she owns. Charm bracelet as in the one she hates. She threw it at my head and knocked me out when I was nine.

HEALY. Do you know the whereabouts of this bracelet?

MELLA (*to the audience*). It's currently holding the kitchen door open. But if I don't tell him that maybe he'll pity me. (*To* HEALY.) I don't, no.

HEALY. Right well. Hopefully it turns up.

MELLA. Yeah. (*Gives the audience a look. Back to* HEALY.) I currently live in the apartment. Do I have any rights to it?

HEALY. Not really.

MELLA. Which means?

HEALY. You have no rights, no.

MELLA. Okay.

HEALY. Are you a religious woman, Mella?

MELLA. I am. Very. (*To the audience*.) I'm not.

HEALY. Oh good. The church can be very comforting at a time like this. Seek forgiveness in God.

MELLA. Seek forgiveness? I haven't done anything.

HEALY. Read the Bible, you probably have.

MELLA. Right.

HEALY. Can I offer you a drink?

MELLA. What?

HEALY. Not here. Maybe elsewhere. Somewhere fancy.

MELLA. I'm not really dressed for it.

HEALY. You don't have to be.

MELLA. No thank you. I'll be busy. Grieving.

HEALY. If you change your mind here's my card. I've put my personal phone number there.

HEALY *slips his card into her breast pocket. She leaves.*

MELLA. Thank you. (*To the audience*.) Slime ball.

Four

MAURA. Wake up in the stockroom of the sweet shop. Crisp crumbs, Curly Wurly wrappers, tin foil containers and empty Fanta cans mottle the concrete floor.

We would be excommunicated from the tennis club if they knew I was stealing. Not that it would make a difference to my social life. I don't play tennis and I don't have a social life.

I don't mean to do it. It's just. Taking things makes me calm. It's in my hand one second and in my pocket the next. I don't know what caused it and I don't know how to stop it.

But I do know I need to get him back. My husband. Even if he did sleep with someone else, it takes two to tango, I'm pretty sure I heard someone say once. I'm no angel, I never said I was. I need to fix this. No more stealing, no more binge eating. I'm going to get slim. I'm going to get slim and make some friends. Yay.

I search 'slimming groups nearby' online. The first result I get is in the church around the corner. Fat Watch. Sounds militant. I like militant.

There's a meeting in thirty minutes. Pull on a fresh twinset, comb my hair and go.

MELLA. So, dead Nanny, no home and no money. Amazing. Nowhere to go so I just start walking. After awhile I see I'm nearly at the church.

MAURA. I get to the door of the church and suddenly I'm terrified I'll see someone I know. Breathe. Strength. Confidence.

MELLA. The church can be very comforting at a time like this. Should I?

MAURA. There's a massive group of women inside. I am a strong confident woman.

MELLA. What's my plan here? Pray for money? Actually that's not a bad plan.

MAURA. An old old buxom lady is corralling new members.

GHOST OF DOLLY PARTON. New fat lady? Good. Up the aisle, top pew, one leaflet each. Next?

MAURA (*to the audience*). I'm next.

GHOST OF DOLLY PARTON. New fat lady?

MAURA. Pardon?

GHOST OF DOLLY PARTON. Are you a fat lady who is new?

MAURA. New?

GHOST OF DOLLY PARTON. New to the group. A new fat lady.

MAURA. Yes I'm new.

GHOST OF DOLLY PARTON. Good. Up the aisle, top pew, one leaflet each. Next?

MAURA. I sit in the front pew.

MELLA. I get to the door, Jesus, church has gone very popular.

A very old, very large-breasted woman asks if I'm a new fat lady. I hear myself tell her –

(*To* GHOST OF DOLLY PARTON.) I'm here as research for my book. Yeah, that's right. I'm an author.

(*To the audience*.) She squeals with excitement, hands me a leaflet that says 'Fat Watch' and tells me I need to sit in the front pew. Ah, it's a slimming group. Okay. Interesting.

MAURA. A girl sits beside me, she smells like chips.

MELLA. I just realised I stink of vinegar from the pre-solicitor chipper I had.

MAURA. God, I'd love chips right now. There are a lot of people here.

MELLA. Maybe this is who I'm supposed to be?

MAURA. Am I a strong confident woman?

MELLA. A slim person, who loves slimming groups.

MAURA. I wonder does everyone know why I'm here?

MELLA. Maybe I'll run a slimming group.

MAURA. So do they think I think I'm fat?

MELLA. Yeah, I'll marry the man in the group, that guy.

MAURA. Or do they know I'm fat and think I just realised?

MELLA. We can have a slimming wedding. And slimming children.

MAURA. I'm not comfortable here, I feel exposed.

MELLA. The girl beside me starts to breathe strangely. Shit, can she smell the vinegar?

MAURA. I'm getting very hot. The woman beside me is looking at me wide-eyed.

MELLA. Don't tell the slimming people I had chips.

MAURA. She looks so freaked out.

MELLA *and* MAURA *look at each other for a moment.*

MELLA. Hey.

MAURA. Hi.

Back to the audience.

Ugh. 'Hi.'

MELLA. I'm rumbled.

MAURA. Everyone shuffles to sit.

MELLA. There are two women left standing.

FAT WATCH LEADER B (*English*) *speaks over the end of* FAT WATCH LEADER A*'s* (*Irish*) *sentences at the* /

FAT WATCH LEADER A. Welcome now, everyone, to group today.

FAT WATCH LEADER B. Yes welcome, everyone, you're very welcome to group today.

FAT WATCH LEADER A. Today we have Charlotte from Fat Watch / HQ.

FAT WATCH LEADER B. I'm Charlotte from Fat Watch HQ, just dropping in today.

FAT WATCH LEADER A. She's just observing our group /
today.

FAT WATCH LEADER B. Just over having a quick look see
how your group runs.

FAT WATCH LEADER A. But don't worry she's not
exa/mining you.

FAT WATCH LEADER B. Oh no gosh I'm not examining you
but I am /

FAT WATCH LEADER A. She's not in charge /

FAT WATCH LEADER B. / over to see why you're not losing
weight /

FAT WATCH LEADER A. / we are losing weight and I am still
in charge /

FAT WATCH LEADER B. / Deborah is in charge of course
but I /

FAT WATCH LEADER A. / I'm still the boss /

FAT WATCH LEADER B. / Am very much Deborah's superior.

Pause.

FAT WATCH LEADER A. Will we get / started now?

FAT WATCH LEADER B. Absolutely get started now.

FAT WATCH LEADER A. Alright today /

FAT WATCH LEADER B. Today, guys.

Pause.

FAT WATCH LEADER A. Actually can I talk to you outside /
please?

FAT WATCH LEADER B. Just going to have a quick word
outside, with Deborah, okay, gang? Faaat Watch.

FAT WATCH LEADER A *and* FAT WATCH LEADER B
leave making faces at each other.

MELLA *and* MAURA *glance at each other.*

MAURA. Two minutes after they've left the volume in the
room starts to rise.

MELLA. Everyone seems to know each other.

MAURA. All nodding and shaking and gasping.

BITCH A *and* BITCH B *start talking*.

BITCH A. I don't believe it.

BITCH B. I couldn't believe it.

BITCH A. Shut. The front. Fuck.

BITCH B. I couldn't actually believe it.

BITCH A. How many did she eat?

BITCH B. Eighteen cakes.

BITCH A. Full cakes?

BITCH B. Full cakes yeah.

BITCH A. In one sitting?

BITCH B. In one mouthful, Mairead.

BITCH A. My god.

BITCH B. I know.

BITCH A. I heard she ate twenty-seven sausages.

BITCH B. She did.

BITCH A. And a wheel of cheese.

BITCH B. I think so.

BITCH A. And a whole child.

BITCH B. A child?

BITCH A. I don't know, probably.

BITCH B. Jesus Christ, sure that has to be illegal.

BITCH A. I think it is, so it is.

BITCH B. How is she still losing weight?

BITCH A. Surgery.

BITCH B. Abortion?

BITCH A. Lipo.

BITCH B. Oh yeah I heard she got lipo.

BITCH A. I heard she got a facelift.

BITCH B. I heard she got her entire stomach removed.

BITCH A. Some people are so sad, so they are.

BITCH B. They are.

> MAURA *and* MELLA *speak to the audience.*

MAURA. The leaders have been outside for ages. Fuck's /

MELLA. Sake. What are they doing out there?

MAURA. I feel uncomfortable.

MELLA. I'm getting hot.

MAURA. This is bollox.

MELLA. This is bullshit.

MAURA. The chip girl keeps looking at me.

MELLA. She can definitely smell the vinegar.

MAURA. Please stop looking at me.

MELLA. She knows I'm lying.

MAURA. Feel like I'm going to vomit.

MELLA. I'll cut her off /

MAURA. But instead out comes /

MELLA (*to* MAURA). Will you ever

TOGETHER (*to each other*). Fuck off.

> LEADERS *come back in the room.*

> *There are no gaps between* FAT WATCH LEADER A *and* FAT WATCH LEADER B*'s following lines.*

FAT WATCH LEADER A. Hi, girls. We got that all sorted now.

> *Pause.* FAT WATCH LEADER B *nods.*

FAT WATCH LEADER B. Sorry, ladies, about that.

FAT WATCH LEADER A. I think we can crack on now.

FAT WATCH LEADER B. We can crack on ahead.

FAT WATCH LEADER A. With Charlotte in the background of the group.

FAT WATCH LEADER B. In the background but also very much up top.

FAT WATCH LEADER A. We have some new members with us today.

FAT WATCH LEADER B. New members, new members here we are.

FAT WATCH LEADER A. Can you stand up and say your names please?

FAT WATCH LEADER B. Say your name, say your name. Please and thanks, guys.

MAURA. Maura.

MELLA. Emily.

FAT WATCH LEADER A. You're both very welcome, Maura and Emily.

FAT WATCH LEADER B. Welcome welcome, Maurha and Emily.

FAT WATCH LEADER A. We'll just do a quick rundown of the facets of Fat Watch.

FAT WATCH LEADER B. Just a small run-through of all the facts about our lovely group.

FAT WATCH LEADER A. This is a warm supportive group.

FAT WATCH LEADER B. You have to come to group every week.

FAT WATCH LEADER A. We have an optimised weight-management plan.

FAT WATCH LEADER B. Y'gotta to weigh yourself in front of everyone.

FAT WATCH LEADER A. Delicious meal plans.

FAT WATCH LEADER B. No chocolate, no alcohol, no sauce.

FAT WATCH LEADER A. Well, not exactly.

MELLA (*simultaneously*). No sauce?

MAURA (*simultaneously*). No sauce?

FAT WATCH LEADER B. Yeah and actually no talking when someone else is talking. It's just rude.

   MELLA *and* MAURA *whisper to each other.*

MELLA. Do you like sauce?

MAURA (*nodding*). Yeah. It's brilliant. Do you like it?

MELLA (*nodding*). Yeah. It is brilliant.

MAURA (*simultaneously*). Sorry for earlier.

MELLA (*simultaneously*). Sorry for telling you to fuck off.

   Brief pause.

MAURA. I'm Maura.

MELLA. I'm Mella.

MAURA. I thought your name was Emily.

MELLA. No. I said it wrong.

MAURA. Oh.

   (*To the audience.*) They pair us together. Mella and me.

MELLA. They put us together.

MAURA. We have to swap numbers.

MELLA. I give her my real number.

MAURA. We read our leaflets.

MELLA. She explains what quinoa is.

MAURA. We can have one cheat meal a week.

MELLA. I suggest we have it together.

MAURA. She asks me to lunch.

MELLA. No idea why I did that.

MAURA. Tell her I'd love to but /

MELLA. She says no.

MAURA. I have to go to work.

MELLA (*to* MAURA). Okay. Of course. Maybe next week?

MAURA (*to* MELLA). Sure.

Five

MAURA (*to the audience*). Leave the church smiling and I realise I didn't think about Philip once. Fat Watch Peanut butter bars in my pocket. I hope no one saw me take them. Back to the sweet shop and Bollocky Bollock is here already. Siobhan 'Snake Eyes' Brady. The biggest mouth in all of Dún Chaoin. She works in the sweet shop with me. Married to misery and having a full-blown affair with gossip, the woman has no rock bottom. She'll tell you which priest is a paedo, which husband is a dog, which toddler is gay and which twelve-year-old girl might be giving blow jobs in the back field. I can't humiliate Philip further. She will eat this up like it's her last meal and ask for seconds. Okay, don't tell her about the sex, don't tell her about the sex, don't tell her about the sex.

Hi Siobhan!

SIOBHAN. Maura, you're in early, what's wrong, what happened, who died?

MAURA. Oh nothing. I'm great thanks, Siobhan, Philip had sex with someone else.

SIOBHAN. Sorry?

MAURA (*to the audience*). Ah, fudge.

SIOBHAN. He what?

MAURA. Is it warm out today?

SIOBHAN. Your husband?

MAURA. Or is it cold?

SIOBHAN. Your husband Philip?

MAURA. Jesus, I can't tell at all.

SIOBHAN. Your husband Philip had sex with someone else? Proper sex? Full sex? Penatrative sex?

MAURA. Penetrative, yes.

SIOBHAN *is delighted. She is beside herself.*

SIOBHAN. Oh my god. How do you know?

MAURA. I don't think I really want to talk about it.

SIOBHAN. Bullshit. Times like these you need to talk.

MAURA. I'd love to not talk.

SIOBHAN. Talk to Siobhan.

MAURA. Yeah, I'll be alright.

SIOBHAN. Siobhan can help.

MAURA. I'll be grand.

SIOBHAN. If you don't let it out you might explode and shoot up a school.

MAURA. I'm not going to do that. Statistically.

SIOBHAN. You might set Philip on fire, if you don't talk about it.

MAURA. There's not a lot to say.

SIOBHAN. Well, let's start with how you found out. Was it recently?

MAURA. Very recently yes.

SIOBHAN (*so delighted*). Oh gosh, that's so awful. How?

MAURA. It was fairly obvious.

SIOBHAN. Was it? What was it? Perfume on the neck? Lipstick on the collar?

MAURA. No.

SIOBHAN. No? Joined a gym? Unexplained spending? New number on a phone bill?

MAURA. Not exactly, no, it was /

SIOBHAN. Don't tell me. I'll get it.

MAURA (*pause*). Okay.

SIOBHAN. Coded texts? Condoms in the car? Obvious lies?

MAURA. Eh /

SIOBHAN. Ah. Let me guess I said.

MAURA. Alright. (*To the audience*.) What is going on?

SIOBHAN. Okay. Extra grooming? Business trips? Leaving the house early with a hat on but returning with no hat?

MAURA. He doesn't have a hat.

SIOBHAN. Okay but don't tell me, Maura. Just don't do it.

MAURA. I won't.

SIOBHAN. I'll get this. I'll get them, I always get them.

MAURA. What?

SIOBHAN. Secretive picture messages? Less sex? No sex? Wanking in the bathroom?

MAURA. Now that I think about it /

SIOBHAN. Prickliness? Evasiveness? Defensiveness?

MAURA. He's always like that but that's not how I found out.

SIOBHAN. Well, what was it for fuck's sake, Maura, you stupid whore?

MAURA. Whoa.

SIOBHAN. Sorry.

MAURA. Yeah.

SIOBHAN. Sorry. I get very hot sometimes. Please tell me how you figured it out. I will literally die if you don't tell me.

MAURA. There wasn't a lot to figure out. I saw him.

SIOBHAN. Oh of course. Surprise visits. You came home unexpectedly. Saw him through a window? Typical.

MAURA. No no, I woke up and he was having sex with someone in our bed.

SIOBHAN. You woke up? Had you blacked out on the floor or something?

MAURA. No I was asleep in the bed.

SIOBHAN. Fuck off.

MAURA. Siobhan.

SIOBHAN. Sorry. (*Pause.*) Well, my god. Who knew he had it in him?

MAURA. I'm starting to think I might have known.

SIOBHAN. Such a pity. Because he is very wealthy.

MAURA. He is, yeah.

SIOBHAN. And yee do have that lovely house together.

MAURA. Yeah.

SIOBHAN. Does he pay the mortgage on it, though? Because you've no money.

MAURA. He doesn't have to, it was my dad's house.

SIOBHAN. Oh that's right, I forgot your dad is dead.

MAURA. What?

SIOBHAN. Your dad. He's dead. And you never knew your mum. So you have no family either.

MAURA. That's right. God, thanks for reminding me.

SIOBHAN. Philip is all you really have, isn't he?

MAURA (*to the audience*). Is she sad or turned on?

SIOBHAN. You don't think anything could be patched up?

MAURA. I don't know.

SIOBHAN. Because you actually don't have any friends either, do you? God, how does a woman of your age make friends anyway?

MAURA (*to the audience*). Okay that's it. (*To* SIOBHAN.)
  Actually I do have a friend, Siobhan.

SIOBHAN. Oh yah? Who's your pal?

MAURA. Her name is Emily, no Mella.

SIOBHAN. I'm sure it is.

MAURA. I met her at my Fat Watch meeting.

SIOBHAN. OH. You're in that slimming group that meets in
  the church?

MAURA. Yes I am. With my friend. Mella.

SIOBHAN. Well. Good for you. Yah it's supposed to be
  amazing, my sister lost seven stone on it.

MAURA. Jesus, your sister didn't need to lose seven stone.

SIOBHAN. I know, she's in the hospital now, but she looks great.

MAURA. Oh my god.

SIOBHAN. She can wear anything, I hate her.

MAURA. Is she okay?

SIOBHAN. She's fab! God, I would absolutely go to Fat Watch
  except I don't need to because my figure is so good.

MAURA. Of course.

SIOBHAN. You should bring your friend into the shop some
  time.

MAURA. Thanks, Siobhan, I absolutely will – (*To the
  audience*.) not.

Six

MELLA (*to the audience*). I shouldn't have said my name was
    Emily. I look weird now. I don't do it on purpose, it's just
    easier to lie sometimes. That way I don't have to be myself
    for a bit.

Got a text from Paddy during Fat Watch asking to meet him
    in the church in an hour. Funeral arrangements. I duck into a
    confession box after the meeting and wait for the slimming
    people to leave. I hear Paddy greet the priest. Father
    Desmond a man constantly just back from /

FATHER DESMOND. Two weekth in Greeth, beautiful
    country.

MELLA (*to the audience*). In fairness, not even a whiff of
    creepiness do I get off the man, although everyone says he's
    lamping it into the gossipy one who works in the newsagent's.
    Paddy has his fat digits gripped around the priest's hand so
    tight it's cutting off circulation for both of them.

PADDY. She was an angel, Father, runs in the family.

MELLA (*to the audience*). I slip into a trance thinking about how
    their fingers look like sausages. If they popped, the loose
    sausage meat would come oozing out and the four hands
    shaking would be one enormous meatball. Then they start to
    look like short, fat penises, floating up and down. Can't get
    that image out of my mind so I ask the Father Desmond:

(*To* FATHER DESMOND.) Can I use your bathroom please,
    Father Desmond?

He points into his chambers. When I lock the door behind
    me, I see Jesus Christ is staring back. This isn't the worst
    thing in the world because on this particular crucifix Jesus is
    sort of meaty. And tanned. One hand in my knickers I lean
    against the door and close my eyes. Maura's face pops into
    my head. Okay. Interesting. The priest knocks at the door.

FATHER DESMOND. Everything all right, Maolíotha?

MELLA. Yes, Father. Fine, Father. (*To the audience*.) Jesus, that
    kind of works for me.

FATHER DESMOND. Thure, take all the time you need.

MELLA. Just about finished, Father.

(*To the audience*.) When I do finish, I feel the guilt set in that every Catholic feels after having a wank in a priest's bathroom.

Paddy says he'll give me a lift home but stops his car at the end of the road and tells me to get out. (*To* PADDY.) Thanks.

PADDY. You're very welcome.

MELLA (*to the audience*). Prick.

PADDY. Mella, I was going to do this over email but I might as well tell you we'll be showing the apartment next week. So. Get out.

MELLA. What am I supposed to do?

PADDY. Stop moaning?

MELLA. Great advice.

PADDY. I don't know, love. Maybe do a prostitution?

MELLA. That's not funny.

PADDY. Ah it is, yeah, listen, I really have to head. Best of luck with it.

MAURA (*to the audience*). When we finally close the shop, I try hanging back outside so I don't have to walk home with Siobhan but she doesn't leave. She just stares at me unblinkingly. Not wanting her to know I actually have nowhere else to sleep except the stockroom, I tell her I forgot my bag:

(*To* MAURA.) Siobhan, I forgot my bag.

SIOBHAN. Did you? I can get it.

MAURA. No no, I'll get it.

SIOBHAN. You're not supposed to be in there after hours, Maura.

MAURA. I'll be two seconds, you go on.

SIOBHAN. Not after you were caught stealing.

MAURA. That was one time, Siobhan.

SIOBHAN. All those Curly Wurlys in your knickers.

MAURA. I'm just getting my bag.

SIOBHAN. Okay. Goodnight, Maura.

MAURA. Night, Siobhan. (*Quietly.*) You thundering bitch.

SIOBHAN. What?

MAURA. Nothing.

(*To the audience*.) Hide behind the counter till she's gone. Spend thirty delicious minutes thinking about what to order for dinner. Fried rice, crispy shredded chicken, beansprouts, spring rolls, prawn toast, large sweet and sour sauce and curry sauce too. Double sauce. When it arrives, I take all the carton tops off and lay everything out. Start shovelling with the plastic fork they give you. Shovel and shovel until the tin foil containers are empty.

MELLA (*to the audience*). Paddy speeds, swerves to miss a cyclist and he's gone. Fuck I need somewhere to live. Need money. Where do people get money? Or houses? The only job I'm qualified for is looking after my nanny and I obviously wasn't very good at that. What about a loan off a friend? Or scam a friend? Yes. Okay. Need to make a friend.

MAURA (*to the audience*). I get sick in my mouth a bit. Tastes like acid. I burp up a mouthful of undigested rice and chicken. Like a baby. Reach the sink just in time to projectile vomit my entire meal.

MELLA. Maura. Maura was nice. Maura looked like she had money. She had a rich-person look. Like she might own or know a horse. Okay. Make a friend, then scam her. I'll tell her I have a lucrative investment opportunity in a horse company. Or that I'm dying. She might let me move in with her. Give her a text, ask her out for a drink. Casual.

MAURA. Pick up my phone and check to see when my husband was last online, three minutes ago. Has he put up any pictures? He has. He's out. With a girl. A young girl. All limbs and tanned skin. He's right, I'm a disgrace. I'm a thief. A fat thief. I don't have any friends. I want to call him but just then my phone beeps.

MELLA. 'Hi Maura, it's Mella here. From Fat Watch. Would you like to meet for a drink tonight? No bother if not, but might be fun to hang out?'

Just as I regret the question mark, I see she's typing.

Seven

Music plays – (Ref. Run the Jewels – 'Close Your Eyes') and actors move toward their meeting point. Music cuts once they start to speak.

MELLA *and* MAURA *speak to each other.*

MAURA. Hey.

MELLA. Hi again.

MAURA. Nice to see you.

MELLA. Gice to see you.

MAURA. What?

MELLA. Good to see you.

MAURA. Okay.

MELLA (*to the audience*). Shit.

MAURA (*to the audience*). Should we hug? I always see girls hugging.

MELLA. How was the rest of your day?

MAURA. Good.

MELLA. Great.

Pause.

Would you like to go inside?

MAURA. It's very busy.

MELLA. Oh. We could go to one of the other pubs?

MAURA. They're all very busy.

MELLA. It's Friday night, the whole town is out.

MAURA. Could we go somewhere else?

MELLA. Are you avoiding someone?

MAURA. I'm avoiding everyone.

MELLA. Ah. Not a people person?

MAURA. Not really.

MELLA. Me neither.

MAURA. Good.

MELLA. We could go back to my apartment?

MAURA. Yes. That sounds nice. Do you want to get food first?

MELLA. Sure.

MELLA (*to the audience*). We hit the chipper.

MAURA. The Hummer Mooney behind the counter. Big belly and oozing oil from every pore.

THE HUMMER. Well, if it isn't the gerls.

MAURA. Hiya, Hummer.

MELLA. You know Hummer?

THE HUMMER. Course she does, she's in here every second night.

MAURA. Ahaha.

THE HUMMER. Maura, garlic cheese chips extra sauce?

MAURA. Yes please.

THE HUMMER. Sound sound not a bother. Mella, bun burger, chips extra vinegar?

MELLA. Drown the fuckers, Hummer.

MAURA. Thanks, Hummer.

THE HUMMER. Sound sound not a bother. Here, Maura, thank yer aul lad for me, will ye?

MAURA. Course. Why?

THE HUMMER. He helped our Lorraine last week. She wants to do the law when she goes to university.

MAURA. Lorraine? (*To the audience*.) I thought I recognised the blonde mop. (*To* THE HUMMER.) I thought she was already in college.

THE HUMMER. No no, school still.

MAURA. School?

THE HUMMER. Convent school up the road. Captain of the debate team so she is.

MAURA. Convent school?

THE HUMMER. Here you go, the gerls.

MAURA. Thanks, The Hummer. Let's go.

THE HUMMER. Sound sound, girls. Not a bother. Mind yourselves.

MELLA. Who's Lorraine?

MAURA. His daughter.

MELLA. And who's your aul lad?

MAURA. My husband.

MELLA. Oh you're married?

MAURA. Let's go.

MELLA. Are you okay?

MAURA. I'm grand, yeah. Can we go to the shops? (*To the audience*.) She's in school.

MELLA. Sure what do you need?

MAURA. Just some food, loot. I need more food. (*To the audience*.) I need to not be in my head for a few minutes.

MELLA. Okay.

Possible music plays – (Ref. Kojaque – 'Flu Shot').

(*To the audience*.) So we hit the big shop.

MAURA. To get food.

MELLA. And drink.

MAURA. And food.

MELLA. In the crisp aisle.

MAURA. In the biscuit aisle.

MELLA. Go to ask her. (*To* MAURA.) Here, prawn cocktail or smoky bacon?

MAURA. Stupid question. Both.

MELLA. When I see her slip a sleeve of extra-value Jaffa Cakes in her bag.

MAURA. I see her see me.

MELLA. Neither of us move.

MAURA. Until I wink.

MAURA *does an enormous wink.*

MELLA. It's disconcerting.

MAURA. And she nods.

MELLA. So I nod.

MAURA. She gets it.

MELLA. I think I get it.

MAURA. Then it's like we're dancing.

MELLA. I sashay up to the security guard /

MAURA. I move to the frozen pizza section /

MELLA. / tell him I've lost my watch,

MAURA. / stick three deep dish in the bag.

MELLA. / say it's a family heirloom,

MAURA. / Garlic dip, hot sauce, salsa, hummus.

MELLA. / and turn on the waterworks.

MAURA. Pack of sour jellies /

MELLA. I have three security guards /

MAURA. A travel Connect Four, I'm going mental.

MELLA. / on their hands and knees looking for this watch.

MAURA. Bottle of red, bottle of whiskey.

MELLA. Up and down the shop.

MAURA. She has half the staff distracted.

MELLA. I start to properly cry. It's amazing.

MAURA. She's wailing.

MELLA. I'm bawling.

MAURA. I don't think they buy it.

MELLA. They bought it.

MAURA. But she makes some scene so it doesn't matter.

MELLA. She nips out the front door, bag and coat bulging.

MAURA. She follows me, ten paces behind.

MELLA. It's like we've done this before.

MAURA. I round a corner and wait for her.

MELLA. I run around and she's waiting for me.

MAURA. She looks so happy.

MELLA. She waited for me.

MAURA. We run back to her apartment.

MELLA. Key in the door.

MAURA. Straight up the stairs.

MELLA. Inside, bags down.

Music swells as they dance in a flurry of adrenaline and celebration. The dance is slick and synchronised. Suddenly music cuts and lights up and we see them shuffle awkwardly around the stage. We realise the slick dance was in their heads.

Eight

MAURA. That was mental.

MELLA. Mental.

MAURA. You're really good at that.

MELLA. You're really good at what you did.

MAURA. What will we eat first?

MELLA. Chips first. Then pizza.

MAURA. Saucy pizza.

MELLA. So do you do that a lot? (*To the audience*.) I'm trying to be sound so she'll like me. Sound and sexy. Why am I trying to be sexy?

MAURA. Not a lot. (*To the audience*.) I do that every day, I'm banned from most shops.

MELLA. Impressive. (*To the audience*.) How do you make friends with someone?

MAURA. Thank you.

Pause.

Who do you live here with?

MELLA. My nanny. But she's dead.

MAURA *laughs,* MELLA *joins in.*

No sorry, she is actually dead.

MAURA. Oh Jesus sorry.

MELLA. No it's fine.

MAURA. Sorry.

MELLA. It's grand.

MAURA. When did she?

MELLA. Em, today.

MAURA. Jesus.

MELLA. She was old. I'm fine.

MAURA. Are you alright?

MELLA. I'm fine.

MAURA (*to the audience*). She doesn't seem fine.

MELLA. I haven't even been to see her.

MAURA. Fuck.

MELLA (*to the audience*). Why did I say that? (*To* MAURA.)
    Where do you live?

MAURA. Hampton Parade.

MELLA. That's around the corner.

MAURA. Yeah.

MELLA. It's really nice.

MAURA. Yeah. Well. I'm not there right now.

MELLA. Oh, did you move?

MAURA. No, I. I had to leave for a bit.

MELLA. Did something happen to your house?

MAURA. No.

MELLA. Are you getting an extension?

MAURA. No.

MELLA. Do you not want to say?

MAURA. No it's okay. My husband had sex with someone else.

MELLA. Oh.

MAURA. In front of me.

MELLA. Oh.

MAURA. Well, beside me, I was in the bed.

MELLA. Jesus. (*Pause*.) Are you alright?

MAURA. I'm fine. He's just under a lot of stress at the moment.

MELLA. Is he?

MAURA. So we're just taking some time.

MELLA. Okay.

MAURA. Nice to have a bit of time.

MELLA *makes a face at the audience*.

Pause.

MAURA. Do you want to play Connect Four?

MELLA. I do. But this one's called Four in a Row. For legal reasons.

MAURA. Duly noted.

MELLA. Can I be red?

MAURA. You can.

Pause – They play.

MELLA. Do you have a job?

MAURA. I work in the newsagent's?

MELLA. I've never seen you in there.

MAURA. I'm only part-time, not working there long.

MELLA. I've seen the other one in there, the mouthy one.

MAURA. Siobhan? Yeah. Try not to tell her anything.

MELLA. Okay.

MAURA. Do you have a job?

MELLA. Well, I was looking after my nanny.

MAURA. Right, sorry yes.

Pause.

Do you miss your nanny?

MELLA. I don't know yet.

MAURA. Because she died today, of course. (*Pause*.) What was she like?

MELLA. She was. Temperamental.

MAURA. Was she?

MELLA. Yeah. She was sick when I was a child, her brain swelled up and when she got better she was. Mean.

MAURA. Mean?

MELLA. Yeah. Not all the time. You just had to be able for her.

MAURA. Like how?

MELLA. Like, you never knew what mood she'd be in so. You'd have to be fairly sharp. Sometimes, she didn't like if you said good morning. Because, what was so good about your morning? Then other times she didn't mind.

MAURA. She didn't mind if you said good morning?

MELLA. Yeah sometimes she didn't mind at all.

MAURA. Right.

MELLA. I'm pretty sharp, though.

MAURA. Yeah I'm sure.

Pause.

MELLA. Are you being sarcastic?

MAURA. No I was being sincere. I'm sure you are.

MELLA. Oh.

Pause.

Anyway. I was well able for her.

MAURA. What do you mean?

MELLA. I know what to say to keep her calm.

MAURA. What would you say?

MELLA. Anything.

MAURA. Anything?

MELLA. Yeah.

MAURA. Like lie to her?

MELLA. Well. Yeah. You'd have to.

MAURA. About what?

MELLA. I don't know. She'd get really upset when she remembered Michael Collins was dead. So I'd pretend he wasn't. To keep her happy.

MAURA. Why would she think Michael Collins was alive? Surely he was long dead before she was born?

MELLA. She saw the film and thought he was still on the go.

MAURA. Right.

MELLA. Yeah. She took a real shine to Liam Neeson.

MAURA. How would you pretend Michael Collins wasn't dead?

MELLA. Like. Normal things.

MAURA. What normal things?

MELLA. Eh. I'd forge letters from him or leave her the odd voicemails as him.

MAURA. What?

MELLA. One time I got an army uniform and dressed up as, actually, d'ya know what, doesn't matter.

MAURA. You dressed up as Michael Collins for your nanny?

MELLA. No I didn't. That's four.

MAURA. Shit, I didn't see that.

MELLA. Yeah well. Eyes up.

MAURA. So you lie to keep people happy?

MELLA. No. I don't lie to keep people happy. It's just easier sometimes.

MAURA. How is it easier?

MELLA. It just is. I don't want to have uncomfortable conversations.

MAURA. Like what for example?

MELLA. Why are you asking?

MAURA. I'm trying to understand.

Pause.

MELLA. Like when my nanny was too drunk to collect me from school. I'd tell the teacher she was sick. Or when girls in my class asked where my parents were, I told them they were scientists working in America. It was easier than the truth.

MAURA. What was the truth?

MELLA. They died in a car crash.

MAURA. Oh. (*Pause.*) I'm sorry.

MELLA. You don't need to be sorry.

Pause.

MAURA. In the meeting you said your name was Emily.

MELLA. Yeah. So?

MAURA. Why did you say that?

MELLA. Em. I don't know. (*Pause.*) I'll put on that pizza.

MAURA. Okay.

Nine

MAURA (*to audience*). This is the longest I've spoken to someone besides Siobhan or Philip in years. And they don't really let me speak. Fuck Philip. That girl is in school.

MELLA (*to audience*). Jesus, where did that come from? I'm supposed to be scamming her not telling her the truth. This is not the way to make friends. You do not tell them the truth, you tell them how brilliant you are and they believe it.

MAURA. Everything alright in there?

MELLA. Tip top. Just need to go to the bathroom.

MAURA (*to audience*). I feel like I should leave. I don't know how to make friends, I'm in too deep with the dead granny and the dead parents. But I don't want to leave her. She's so sad. And nice. My heart starts to beat faster. I'm getting very hot. Need to calm myself down. I look over at the kitchen door and see something on the ground. It's a bracelet. It's filthy and the weight of a church.

MELLA. Hey.

MAURA. Hi.

MELLA. Pizza's on.

MAURA. Great.

Pause. Back to Four in a Row.

MELLA. So. What does your husband do?

MAURA. He works in law. Mostly personal finance and taxes but he does trusts and stuff too.

MELLA. Sounds fun. Is he fun?

MAURA. He works hard.

MELLA. Is that fun?

MAURA. He's highly strung.

MELLA. Does he know you're so good at stealing?

Pause.

MAURA. He is aware, yes.

MELLA. How much have you stolen?

MAURA. A few bits.

MELLA. What's your barometer?

MAURA. How many lies have you told?

MELLA. Impossible to quantify. You're in trouble here.

MAURA. Are you trying to be funny?

MELLA. No I have three in a row.

MAURA. You shouldn't have told me.

MELLA. It was getting embarrassing.

MAURA. You're not funny.

MELLA. I am a bit.

MAURA. You're not.

MELLA. Ah I am, though.

MAURA. Yeah? Who told you that?

MELLA. No one, I can just feel it.

MAURA. You haven't made me laugh.

MELLA. Yeah but maybe you just have a terrible sense of humour.

MAURA. Maybe.

Pause.

MELLA. Is your husband not nice?

MAURA. That's a very personal question.

MELLA. Is it?

MAURA. Yes. Your grandmother doesn't sound very nice.

MELLA. She was sick. It wasn't her fault.

Pause.

MAURA. I don't know if my husband is very nice.

MELLA. No?

MAURA. But I don't think it's his fault.

MELLA. No?

MAURA. He's never done anything in particular /

MELLA. Until he slept with someone else in front of you?

MAURA. Until that. Yes. In general, I just feel worse around him.

Pause.

MELLA. What does he do?

MAURA. Em. I don't know. I do think it might be my fault.

MELLA. Right.

MAURA. Yeah.

MELLA. Why do you think that?

MAURA. Well. Em. Early on, when we started seeing each other, he lost his watch. It was very expensive. We looked everywhere for it, retraced his steps. Couldn't find it. A week later, he found it. In my bag.

MELLA. He found it?

MAURA. He did.

MELLA. Did you take it?

MAURA. Yes. Well, I must have. But I have no memory of taking it.

MELLA. Oh.

MAURA. I was so embarrassed.

MELLA. Of course.

MAURA. He was angry at first, but he forgave me.

MELLA. That was nice of him.

MAURA. It was. He is. (*Referring to the game.*) There.

MELLA. Oh. I didn't see that.

MAURA. Sneaky diagonal.

MELLA. Is that why you think it's your fault?

MAURA. Em. Well, it kept happening. Can I be red now?

MELLA. Sure. What kept happening?

MAURA. Things kept going missing.

MELLA. What things? You go first, because you won.

MAURA. Great.

MELLA. What things went missing?

MAURA. Other things. His money, credit cards, car keys, his phone.

MELLA. You were stealing from him?

MAURA. Actually I have no memory of taking anything from him. It was just after my father died and I was in a bit of a state. I was so grateful he didn't leave me.

MELLA. I'm sorry your dad is dead.

MAURA. It's fine, he's dead years now.

Pause.

(*Referring to the game.*) You're good at this.

MELLA. Do you remember what you just stole?

MAURA. Today?

MELLA. At the shop yeah.

MAURA. Yeah, of course.

MELLA. But you don't remember stealing anything back then?

MAURA. No.

MELLA. Did you ever think, the times you don't remember, were him?

MAURA. No, I don't. (*Pause.*) Why would he do that?

MELLA. To make you want to stay with him?

MAURA. He hardly needed to do that. He is a bit out of my league.

MELLA. What do you mean?

MAURA. You know what I mean.

MELLA. What?

MAURA. He's handsome and very successful. And I'm a whale.

MELLA. No you're not.

Pause.

Four.

MAURA. What?

MELLA. Four.

MAURA. Oh.

MELLA. Yeah.

MAURA. Sugar.

MELLA. Do you want to get back with him?

MAURA. I'm going to try.

MELLA. Really?

MAURA. Why are you asking about my husband?

MELLA (*to the audience*). Shit. (*To* MAURA.) I don't know, I'm just trying to get to know you and be your friend.

MAURA (*to the audience*). Shit. (*To* MELLA.) Well, I'm glad to hear that because I want to be your friend too.

Pause.

MELLA (*to the audience*). So we talk.

MAURA (*to the audience*). For hours.

MELLA. For ages.

MAURA. It's amazing.

MELLA. She thinks I'm funny.

MAURA. She is funny.

MELLA. She makes me laugh.

MAURA. She's a weird laugh.

MELLA. We eat the pizza.

MAURA. Drink the wine.

MELLA. Play Four in a Row.

MAURA. She's really good at it.

MELLA. She talks about Philip.

MAURA. I tell her about Philip.

MELLA. How he pays for everything.

MAURA. But not about Lorraine.

MELLA. But he doesn't let her forget it.

MAURA. How he looks after me.

MELLA. How he takes her wages.

MAURA. How we have a joint bank account.

MELLA. Which she has no card for.

MAURA. How he's never hit me.

MELLA. He just embarrasses her.

MAURA. How I miss him.

MELLA. She misses him.

MAURA. How I want him back.

MELLA. But he fucked someone else.

MAURA. But it was only once.

MELLA. And he sounds mental.

MAURA. We talk about her apartment.

MELLA. How Paddy's going to sell it.

MAURA. He sounds like a prick.

MELLA. He's such a prick.

MAURA. About her not having any money.

MELLA. Tell her all I was left is a charm bracelet.

MAURA. The charm bracelet that was holding open the door.

MELLA. Feel bad for wanting to scam her.

MAURA. I think I'd like to stay with her.

MELLA. Why is her husband so mean?

MAURA. I don't know if she'd want me to.

MELLA. She could stay here tonight.

MAURA. Wish I could stay here.

MELLA. Feel like asking her.

MAURA. We put music on.

MELLA. But I don't.

MAURA. We laugh.

MELLA. We dance.

MAURA. We eat.

MELLA. And drink.

MAURA. And dance.

MELLA. And dance. Then she does it.

MAURA. I ask about her love life.

MELLA. Fuck it.

MAURA. Is she seeing anyone?

MELLA. I've never seen anyone.

MAURA. Is she straight?

MELLA. I don't know.

MAURA. She's squirming.

MELLA. She'll think I'm a freak.

MAURA. Have I said something wrong?

MELLA. She's married, she won't want to be friends with
    a virgin.

Ten

MAURA. Sorry we don't have to talk about that.

MELLA. No it's fine, I'm just not seeing anyone at the moment.

MAURA. Okay. Girls or boys?

MELLA (*pause*). Both?

MAURA. Really?

MELLA. Mmmhmm.

MAURA (*to the audience*). Fuck this is awkward. (*To* MELLA.) When was the last time?

MELLA (*to the audience*). Fuck I have to lie. (*To* MAURA.) Eh actually. Today.

MAURA. Today?

MELLA. Yeah. Today. I had sex today.

MAURA. Wow. With who?

MELLA. My solicitor.

MAURA. Your solicitor? Where?

MELLA. In his office.

MAURA. Wow.

MELLA. It was wow.

MAURA. How was it?

MELLA. Greasy.

MAURA. What?

MELLA. Sweaty?

MAURA. Amazing. Are you seeing him?

MELLA. Not really, it just happened. When we were going over the will.

MAURA. Your nanny's will?

MELLA. Yeah. It was. Hot.

MAURA. What's his name?

MELLA. Eh.

MELLA *pats herself down, looking for the card* HEALY *gave her. She finds it in her breast pocket and checks it.*

Phil Healy.

MAURA. Sorry?

MELLA *hands the card to* MAURA.

MELLA. Phil Healy.

MAURA. Philip Healy?

MELLA. Yeah I guess.

MAURA. You fucked Philip Healy today?

MELLA. Yes. I did. Why do you know him?

MAURA. No.

MELLA. Okay. Yeah it was a one-off, don't think it'll happen again.

MAURA (*to the audience*). Is everyone except me having sex with my husband? I have to get out of here. (*To* MELLA.) Mella, I actually have to go.

MELLA. You're leaving?

MAURA. Yeah I just have to /

MELLA. Are you not having fun?

MAURA. I am. I just feel a bit sick.

MELLA. Where are you staying?

MAURA. Eh.

MELLA. I have a spare bedroom. Would you like to stay here?

MAURA. I can't.

MELLA. Oh. Why?

MAURA. I just can't.

MELLA. Are you sure?

MAURA. Yes.

MELLA. Please?

MAURA. No.

MELLA. Why?

MAURA. Because you fucked my husband.

Pause.

MELLA. What?

MAURA. Philip Healy. The solicitor. He's my husband. I'm
    Maura Healy.

MELLA. Oh no. (*To the audience.*) Oh no.

MAURA. Yeah.

MELLA. No no I didn't have sex with him.

MAURA. You just told me you did. And you have his card.

MELLA. I was lying. I didn't have sex with him.

MAURA. And you expect me to believe you?

MELLA. I promise I didn't, I didn't want you to know /

MAURA. I don't believe you.

MELLA. I didn't want you to know I've never had sex.

MAURA. What?

MELLA. I've never had sex.

MAURA. You're a liar.

MELLA. Yes, technically.

MAURA. How did you know about Philip?

MELLA. He is my solicitor, I just didn't fuck him.

MAURA. Sure.

MELLA. No, seriously.

MAURA. You're a fucking liar.

MELLA. I'm not, I did. I am. But I haven't been lying to you.

MAURA. How am I supposed to trust you now? Did you even
    think about that, Mella?

MELLA. I'm sorry, I'm sorry.

MAURA. You did fuck him.

MELLA. I promise I didn't.

MAURA. I bet you told him to ride you like a road instructor.

MELLA. What?

> MAURA *shoves* MELLA.

> Don't put your hands on me.

> MELLA *shoves* MAURA. *Out of* MAURA*'s pocket falls* MELLA*'s charm bracelet*

MAURA (*to the audience*). Fuck.

MELLA. What's that?

MAURA. Oh?

MELLA. Is that my charm bracelet? (*To the audience.*) It is.

MAURA. Is it? (*To the audience.*) It is.

MELLA. Yeah.

MAURA. How did it get there?

MELLA. Was it in your pocket?

MAURA. Was it?

MELLA. Yes.

MAURA. Did you put it there?

MELLA. No.

MAURA. Oh.

MELLA. Wow.

MAURA. What?

MELLA. You know I didn't put it there.

MAURA. I don't know.

MELLA. You were going to steal it?

MAURA. No.

MELLA. When?

MAURA. Eh.

MELLA. When I put the pizza on?

MAURA. Yeah.

MELLA. I told you about dressing up like Michael Collins for my dead nanny and you choose that moment to steal from me.

MAURA. You did dress up as him, no I'm sorry.

MELLA. You're not sorry. You're a fucking liar. You betrayed me like De Valera betrayed Michael Collins. You're De Valera.

MAURA. Well, I feel betrayed. Like Michael Collins betrayed the North.

MELLA. Stop talking about Michael Collins.

MELLA *shoves* MAURA.

MAURA. You said you had sex with my husband.

MELLA. I didn't but actually I seem to be the only woman in town he hasn't had sex with.

MAURA. He wouldn't have sex with you.

MELLA. He wouldn't have sex with you either.

MAURA. No one wants you, Mella.

MELLA. Fuck off, Maura.

MAURA. No one wants you, no one wants to have sex with you, no one even likes you.

MELLA. Maura, stop.

MAURA. Your family didn't like you.

MELLA. You don't know that.

MAURA. It's true, though.

MELLA. It's not.

MAURA. No one's ever wanted you.

MELLA. They do.

MAURA. You have no family.

MELLA. Stop.

MAURA. No friends.

MELLA. Stop.

MAURA. And you're a fucking liar.

MELLA *raises her hand to hit* MAURA.

Mella.

MELLA *stops*.

Mella.

Pause.

What was that?

MELLA. I don't know.

MAURA. Were you going to hit me?

MELLA. I don't know.

MAURA. You're a disgrace.

MELLA. I'm sorry.

Pause.

MAURA. Okay.

MELLA. Fuck.

MAURA. It's fine.

MELLA. I didn't mean to.

MAURA. It's okay.

MELLA. I'm shit. I feel so shit.

MAURA. I shouldn't have said that about your family.

MELLA. They didn't like me. No one likes me.

MAURA. That's not true. I like you.

MELLA. You don't.

MAURA. Mella, I'm sorry. I shouldn't have said that. You're not a disgrace.

MELLA. I am. I can't stand myself. Every time I pass a reflective surface I check to see if I'm still there. And I'm so disappointed when I see myself.

MAURA. Don't say that.

MELLA. I just wanted you to like me. But I'm horrible.

MAURA *tries to hug* MELLA.

Please don't touch me.

MAURA. I'm exactly like him.

MELLA. You're not.

MAURA. A whale. That's what he calls me.

Pause

Every morning, after he goes to work. I stand in front of the mirror, in my underwear and pull at bits of my body I want to cut off. I want to get a knife from the kitchen and cut off parts of me.

He doesn't love me. I don't think he ever did. I was just happy someone was paying attention to me.

MELLA. He's a fuck.

MAURA. Yeah.

Pause.

MELLA. I feel so lonely.

MAURA. Me too.

Pause.

I'm sorry I took your bracelet.

MELLA. It's fine. It's a piece of shit.

MAURA. It is.

MELLA. Well, you shouldn't have taken it then.

MAURA. Sorry.

Pause.

MELLA. I'm sorry I lied about having sex with your husband.

MAURA. Did he try to?

MELLA. He just gave me his card.

MAURA. He did try to.

MELLA. I'm sorry.

MAURA. I'm sorry too.

MELLA. Can I get you anything?

MAURA. Would a voice note from Michael Collins be out of the question?

MELLA. Yeah I'll get Liam Neeson right on that.

Pause.

MAURA. Mella, what's the point?

MELLA. Of life?

MAURA. Yeah.

MELLA. I don't know. Laughing?

MAURA. That's a terrible point.

Pause.

MELLA. Maura?

MAURA. Yeah?

MELLA. Can we be friends?

MAURA. Yeah.

MELLA. I won't lie to you again. Promise.

MAURA. Okay. I won't steal from you.

MELLA. Good.

Pause.

Feels like a low bar for a friendship.

MAURA. Yeah well. It's a start.

Pause.

MELLA (*to the audience*). Small and safe South Dublin suburb.

MAURA. Newsagent's where I still work.

MELLA. Chipper where we still eat.

MAURA. And church we don't go into any more.

MELLA. We live in Maura's house now.

MAURA. Paddy sold the apartment.

MELLA. And with the money he bought another apartment.

MAURA. He's such a prick.

MELLA. And Philip was arrested for statutory rape.

MAURA. Arrested and charged.

MELLA. Someone told The Hummer Mooney.

MAURA. He was less than impressed.

MELLA. He was fucking furious.

MAURA. And he called the Guards.

MELLA. So Maura got her dad's house back.

MAURA. We still lie.

MELLA. And steal.

MAURA. But only sometimes.

MELLA. And not to each other.

MAURA. We still get chips with too much sauce.

MELLA. It enhances the flavour.

MAURA. From bland to bliss.

MELLA. We eat them in the church car park.

MAURA. And remember how we told each other to fuck off the first day we met.

MELLA. Let us never forget.

End of play.

ALL HONEY

All honey was first performed at The New Theatre, Dublin, as part of Dublin Fringe Festival, on 10 September 2017, with the following cast and creative team:

RU	Danielle Galligan
LUKE	David Fennelly
MAE	Ashleigh Dorrell
BARRY	Keith Jordan
VAL	Ciara Elizabeth Smyth

Director	Jeda de Brí
Set Designer	Sinéad Purcell
Costume Designer	Ellen Therese Fleming
Lighting Designer	Maggie O'Donovan
Stage Manager	Sionnán Ní Nualláin
Production Assistant	Tamar Keane
Photography	Lorna Fitzsimons
Graphics	Peter Grogan

It was revived at Bewley's Café Theatre, Dublin, on 8 January 2018, with the same cast and creative team, and then at Project Arts Centre, Dublin, on 13 February 2020, with the following cast and creative team:

RU	Clodagh Mooney Duggan
LUKE	Finbarr Doyle
MAE	Ashleigh Dorrell
BARRY	Keith Jordan
VAL	Maeve O'Mahony

Director	Jeda de Brí
Producer	Katie McCann
Set Designer	Sinéad Purcell
Costume Designer	Ellen Therese Fleming
Lighting Designer	Dara Hoban
Photography	Lorna Fitzsimons

Characters

MAE
LUKE
RU
BARRY
VAL

Notes on Text

The play takes place in the box room (spare room) of a flat inhabited by Ru and Luke.

Location: Wherever

Time: Whenever

A dash (–) denotes an interruption by action.

A forward slash (/) denotes overlapping speech or an interruption by another character speaking.

An ellipsis (…) denotes a character trailing off or struggling to find the end of the sentence.

Scene One

Her Nightgown

RU *is unpacking a box hurriedly, looking for something, muttering to herself.* LUKE *enters, slightly flustered and pauses briefly, as if he had forgotten what he came in for. When he opens the door we hear the murmur of people and music from down the hall. A house-warming.*

RU *stops what she is doing and stares at* LUKE. *Buzzer sounds and* LUKE *leaves the room to answer it.* RU *finds what she is looking for, gets up and leaves the room. Stage is empty for about eight seconds. Muffled sound of* RU *and another female talking. Door flies open, in walks* MAE, *who is holding a depleted gin and tonic, followed by* RU.

MAE. The fact is it's happening.

RU. Right.

MAE. I mean, that's just a fact. The fact is. It's happening.

RU. Is it?

MAE. It is. (*Pause.*) I mean, I felt it. He would. Deny. Denied. Everything. I thought I was going out of my mind. In my head he was... at it. Then in the flesh, I was. Accusing him unjustly.

RU. Mmmm.

MAE. But then I found it.

RU. What?

MAE (*whispers*). Her nightgown.

RU. Her nightgown?

MAE. Her nightgown. Can you believe it?

RU. No.

MAE. I know.

RU. That's so strange.

MAE. Isn't it. (*Nodding*.)

Pause.

Is it?

RU. It's just. A nightgown?

MAE. Oh.

RU. Right?

MAE. There's no need to be embarrassed.

RU. Sorry?

MAE. You see, Ru, it's a gown. That you wear. When you sleep. In the night-times.

RU. No no I know what a nightgown is.

MAE. So what's the problem?

RU. You found her nightgown?

MAE. Yes, well.

RU. The woman you think is sleeping with your /

MAE. Yes.

RU. Her nightgown, you found.

MAE. Alright, Ru, can we pick this up please.

RU. My problem is, if this woman is – (*Gesturing*.) with your. Sorry what are we calling him now?

MAE. Barry.

RU. Just Barry?

MAE. My Barry.

Pause.

RU. Okay. If she is, if she has been, with your Barry, in your house. She's not. Staying the night. I mean she wouldn't sleep over.

MAE. No of course not. I live there.

RU. That's right.

MAE. That's where I sleep.

RU. Of course.

MAE. And I don't have a guest room.

RU. You don't.

MAE. What are you getting at, Ru?

RU. So if she's not staying over, in the night-times.

MAE. Because I sleep in my bed.

RU. Because you sleep in your bed. So if she's not staying over in the night-times, because you sleep in your bed. Then why should she need a nightgown?

MAE. Oh yes I see what you're saying.

RU. You do.

MAE. Yes of course. Because they would be engaging in intercourse.

RU. Well. Sex.

MAE. Language, Ru.

RU. And also.

MAE. Hmm?

RU. A nightgown?

MAE. Yes?

RU. Who wears a nightgown?

MAE. Ahm.

RU. I mean, I don't wear a nightgown.

MAE. No.

RU. I sleep naked.

MAE. What?

RU. Nude.

MAE. Right.

RU. So?

MAE (*pause*). I mean. I wear pyjamas.

RU. No!

MAE. What?

RU. You found the nightgown.

MAE. Yes I did!

RU. And what did you think?

MAE. Well, what would you think? If you found a nightgown in Luke's things?

Pause.

RU. The neighbours.

MAE. What?

RU. We share a washing machine. With the neighbours.

MAE. Ru, how is that helpful? I have my own washing machine.

RU. Of course.

MAE. And my own house.

RU. Yep.

MAE. That I bought. That he stays in.

RU. Rent-free. I know, I'm sorry, go on. You found the nightgown.

MAE. Yes. And this nightgown. More than confirmed my suspicions.

RU. I suppose it would.

MAE. It did.

RU. Prick.

MAE. Skirt chaser.

Pause.

RU. Was it. Very sexy?

MAE. It was – (*Remembering.*) horrific.

RU. Oh, Mae.

MAE. It was so frilly. You couldn't move for the frills.

RU. Jesus.

MAE. High neck, long sleeves, floor-length. Baggy too. My god, was it baggy.

RU. Oh. That's sort of different than I /

MAE. I mean I presumed they were playing house or some sick /

RU (*nodding seriously*). Right.

MAE. / thing.

RU. Mmm.

MAE. In nightgowns with Victorian fetish /

RU. Uh.

MAE. / shit.

RU. Mmm.

MAE. All like – (*Makes a face and gestures.*)

RU. Perverts.

MAE (*nodding slowly and inhaling before speaking*). Exactly. (*Pause.*) So I confronted him. 'I smell her off you. You're found out. Caught. In your lies. No fools here, baby.'

RU. Baby?

MAE. No fools! Did you think I wouldn't find out? You scum. The colour drained from his face.

RU. And?

MAE. He crumbled. (*Nodding.*) Buried his face between my legs. Clutched at the back of my thighs. Shaking. Like a…

Silence as both RU *and* MAE *think of an appropriate simile.*

RU. Like a dog?

MAE. Yes. Like a dog. Shaking like a dog. He shook like a dog.

RU. Wow. So he?

MAE. Hmm?

RU. Admitted.

MAE. What? No.

RU. What?

MAE. No.

RU. He didn't?

MAE. I made a mistake. I – (*Pause*.) when he had his face
buried, and I was…

> RU *makes a talking gesture with her hand.*

> You are being so unhelpful.

RU. Sorry.

MAE. When I was, going on. A bit. I mentioned the nightgown.
I said it out. 'I've found her nightgown'. When the last
syllable left my lips. His grip on my thighs loosened. And
I knew I'd made a mistake. 'Nightgown?' He said. And he
said it like that too. 'Nightgown?' Then the laughter started.
That fucked me right off. Then he looked up at me. Tears in
his eyes. But not good tears, not the tears I wanted. Bad
tears, happy tears. 'The nightgown' he said, 'the nightgown
is for my mother.'

RU. What? Was it new?

MAE. Yes.

RU. It had tags?

MAE. Indeed.

RU. In a shopping bag?

MAE. Precisely.

> *Brief pause.*

RU. What?

MAE. That's not important. You see, I caught him.

RU. Did you?

MAE. He broke down. Why did he break down?

RU. Okay. What did you say?

MAE. Nothing. At first. Couldn't believe he was smiling. Then I started. I mean I really got started. I told him he hasn't been showing me any affection. I said to him, 'I'm a success. This is what success looks like. These are the eyes, nose, mouth and ears of success. Quite literally, this is the face of success. And if you think such a success is going to hang around for cold scraps of meat that you try to pass off for affection, think again, baby.'

RU. Baby? Again /

MAE. He apologised. Said he would. Try.

RU. Right. That sounds.

MAE. Yeah.

RU. Did you ask why he got so upset?

MAE. I was out of ammo at that stage. So we went to bed. He was gone when I woke up. And guess what he took with him.

RU. No?

MAE. The nightgown. To work.

RU. When was that?

MAE. Two days ago.

RU. Where is he now?

MAE. He was supposed to meet for dinner and come here together.

RU. And why didn't he?

MAE. He texted. He had to work late. Emergency. Said he'll be here in a few hours.

RU. Jesus.

MAE. I know what you're thinking.

RU. Do you?

MAE. Yes I do. When is Detective Mae going to re-confront that bastard Barry.

RU. I wasn't thinking that at all.

MAE. I'm going to call him out. Again. Tonight. In front of everybody. Genevieve said it would be cathartic.

RU. Genevieve told you to do that? Here?

MAE. She did. She's so smart.

RU. You might like some privacy?

MAE. No I'd like the audience.

RU. Okay, why don't we first get a drink.

MAE. Another one. Yes.

RU. Yes. Another one. And let's have a chat about that option.

They both go to leave, MAE *first. As she exits, enter* LUKE.

LUKE. Ru, oh hi Mae. Having a good time?

MAE (*sarcastically*). Oh yes, Luke. I am having a brilliant time.

Pause.

LUKE. Great. Ru?

RU. Luke?

LUKE. Would you go out and serve please, I just need to…

RU. Sure no problem.

RU *starts looking at* LUKE *with wild eyes and signalling she would like to talk to him.* LUKE *picks up on this.*

LUKE. Eh, Mae?

MAE. Yes, Luke?

LUKE. I think someone. Was, at. Your handbag? All your lady bits are on the floor.

MAE. What?

LUKE. Yeah, all over the place. Someone really got in there. You better go. Have a look.

MAE. Jesus, Luke.

MAE *leaves quickly.* LUKE, *pleased with his quick thinking, turns to* RU.

Scene Two

You Detached Yourself

RU. What was that?

LUKE. I thought you wanted me to get her out.

RU. I did but I didn't want you to say someone robbed her bag.

LUKE. I thought that was good.

RU. It wasn't.

LUKE. Yeah well, I'm not good on the spot and I'm not good at pretending.

RU. I can see that.

LUKE. Is everything okay?

RU. Not really.

LUKE (*looking at his phone*). Right.

RU. Luke.

LUKE (*looking up from his phone*). Sorry, people keep texting me.

RU. We have a problem.

LUKE. Right. Is it /

RU. Barry.

LUKE. What about him?

RU. He's been having an affair.

LUKE. What makes you think that?

RU. Well, Mae thinks that.

LUKE. Oh. I thought they broke up.

RU. They're back together.

LUKE. Really? He didn't, I mean he never. Said.

RU. You were talking to him about it?

LUKE. No, just. You know. We chat. And he never. Mentioned.

RU. Well, they are. But now /

LUKE. When?

RU. When what?

LUKE. Sorry, since when are they back together?

RU. Two weeks.

LUKE. Right.

RU. Am I missing something?

LUKE. No. Sorry no.

RU. You're anxious.

LUKE. No. I'm distracted. I just. He's coming here tonight.

RU. Yeah that's the problem. Did he say anything to you when you were out with him last week?

LUKE. No, Jesus, no.

RU. Right. Well. She's planning a confrontation tonight. Here.

LUKE. Here?

RU. Yes.

LUKE. Who is she confronting?

RU. What? Barry.

LUKE. Yes of course sorry.

Pause.

And who does she. Think he's. Been with.

RU. She doesn't know.

LUKE. She must have some idea.

Brief pause.

RU. Luke, do you have some idea?

LUKE. I don't, Jesus, not at all. It's just. I didn't think we'd have to stop a fight tonight.

RU. I know. She found a nightgown the other night and it's really set her off.

Pause.

LUKE. A nightgown?

RU. A nightgown. She thought it was his lover's. But apparently it was a present for his mother.

LUKE. Right. Where is she now?

RU. Gone to get a drink.

LUKE. You thought that was the best thing? Alcohol?

RU. Yes.

LUKE. You should go out to her.

RU. I will.

> RU *goes to leave and stops before* LUKE *can follow her.*

How is everything out there?

LUKE. Fine yeah.

RU. Are people enjoying themselves?

LUKE. Oh yeah. They seem to be. (*Deadpan.*) Loving it.

RU. Nothing. Strange or wonderful?

LUKE. No. Oh. There's a girl just come in with some serious. (*Searching for the word.*) Eyebrows.

RU. Oh yeah. That's Jessica. From work.

LUKE. Jessica?

RU (*doing an impression of her*). Jessica.

LUKE. Oh, your one.

RU. Yeah.

LUKE. Do you hang round with her?

RU. Yeah, tea break, lunch.

LUKE. She's mental. She just told me she broke up with someone because of the stock market.

RU. Yeah. Did she start to explain how the stock market works?

LUKE. Yes! Ru, I don't want to know how the stock market works.

RU. I know, it's awful.

RU *smiles*.

I love you.

LUKE. I love you too.

Silence.

RU. Do you?

Silence.

LUKE. Of course.

Silence.

RU. Okay. (*Pause*.) Good.

RU *goes to say something but decides not to. Pause*.

You do love me.

LUKE. I do.

RU. Okay. No I know. It's just. You say. Nothing.

LUKE. I… don't?

RU. You don't love me?

LUKE. I do!

RU. Okay. You don't ever say.

LUKE. I just said.

RU. Yeah. But other things. You don't ever say other things. Voluntarily.

LUKE (*kindly*). You're not making sense.

RU. Okay.

LUKE. I do love you. Sweet. Pea.

RU. How much do you love me?

LUKE. Bloody loads.

RU. As much as I love you?

LUKE. Probably.

RU. What?

LUKE. Yes yes.

RU (*under her breath*). Unsettling.

LUKE. Pardon?

RU (*much louder*). That's unsettling.

   Silence.

LUKE. We should go back out.

RU. Why?

LUKE. Because you're getting all. Raaah. You know the way you get.

RU. No.

LUKE. Ah, you do know.

RU. Nope.

LUKE. Ah, you know the way you are.

RU. Are you confident continuing this?

LUKE. No, I'd really like to stop talking.

RU. Good. (*Pause.*) Do you know what, I had a dream last night about you.

LUKE. Did you?

RU. I did. I was outside my old office with the people from my old office and the sun was shining. Like it does. In the summer. Do you remember? It was beside the Liffey. So the sun was shining and hitting the water and I looked down, at the water and the water was blue. Can you believe it? Because it's normally /

LUKE. Yeah.

RU. Green.

LUKE. What?

RU (*louder*). Green.

LUKE. Green.

RU. Yes. Well. I can't remember exactly what I was doing but I was on a mission. Then all of a sudden, I hear an electrical wheelchair.

LUKE. What's that?

RU. An electrical wheelchair.

LUKE. Right. No yeah, that's, that's what I thought you said.

RU. Yeah. (*Pause*.) So I hear an electrical wheelchair. And it's coming at me. Fast. And I looked up and it was you. In the electrical wheelchair. And you were going. So fast. And you flew right past me, in your chair, and you went straight into the water. Then you detached yourself from the chair and swam to the side. You climbed out and ran over to me and said 'I didn't want you to be late.' Isn't that sweet?

LUKE. Is it?

RU. Yeah. You didn't want me to be late.

LUKE. For what?

RU. My mission.

LUKE. Right. (*Pause*.) Sounds like Luke deserves a thank-you.

RU. Yes I would thank you but I think you were having an affair.

LUKE. What?

RU. In the dream. In the dream you were having an affair.

LUKE. What? When?

RU. When what?

LUKE. When was I having an affair on you? I was flying around in a wheelchair.

RU (*remembering*). Oh, you were going so fast.

LUKE. When was I... 'doin it' on you? I was in a wheelchair.

RU. Oh you don't think people in wheelchairs can cheat?

LUKE. No. Logistically.

RU. What?

LUKE. Logistically. Was I 'at it'? When I was in the wheelchair? Was she on my lap?

RU. No, no before that I think.

LUKE. Did you see?

RU. No. I didn't see was just a feeling I got.

LUKE. Was she as good looking as you?

RU. It wasn't with a woman.

LUKE. What?

RU. It wasn't with a woman.

LUKE. Okay. Was he. As good looking as you?

RU. It was a penguin.

LUKE. A what?

RU. A penguin.

LUKE. A penguin?

RU. Yes.

LUKE. I was cheating on you with a penguin?

RU. That's right.

LUKE. But you didn't see any of this.

RU. Correct.

LUKE. You just got the feeling I'd been cheating on you with a penguin before I whizzed past you in an electrical wheelchair that I didn't need?

RU. That was the state of affairs, yes.

LUKE. That's horrible.

RU. I don't think you'd really cheat on me.

LUKE. No.

RU. It was just a dream.

LUKE. No, that you think I'd… force myself upon a penguin.

RU. I don't think you'd force yourself upon a penguin!

LUKE. But you said /

RU. No it was more emotional. Hand holding.

LUKE. They don't have hands. They have /

RU. Yeah.

LUKE. I'd never do that to you.

RU. I don't think you would. Love.

LUKE. Right. Good.

Pause.

Is something wrong?

RU. Yes.

LUKE. Is it the penguin?

RU. No.

LUKE. Oh. What is it? Cup. Cake.

RU. I know you're trying to be affectionate using those names but you just sound hungry.

LUKE. I'm starving.

RU. I spent all day cleaning while you sat there on your phone. And when I asked you to clean the baking tray you threw it in the bin.

LUKE. It was very dirty, though.

RU. That's why I asked you to clean it. Luke, you can't spend all day looking at your phone. We're together all the time now. You have to talk to me.

LUKE. Okay. I didn't realise I was. I'm sorry.

RU. Okay. Let's go outside.

LUKE. Hang on, where is the thing that holds the dip? That's what I came in for. Some guys from your work just came in. They brought parfait.

RU. Pâté or parfait?

LUKE. What's the difference?

RU. Luke, come on.

LUKE. Okay?

RU. Are they *all* here? The dip thing is in the small box.

LUKE. Oh. Good. Not all of them, are they all coming? And where's the thing that holds the thing that holds the dip?

RU. They are. It's in the big box.

LUKE. Where is it?

RU. In there. It should be right on top.

LUKE. Ehh.

RU. It's right there.

LUKE (*talking over her*). It's right where? Here?

RU. Yes.

LUKE. Oh right, no yes I mean the other thing.

RU. Oh, that broke.

LUKE. Oh.

RU. Yeah. There should be another thing, though.

LUKE. Forget it. Are your friends from fencing coming?

RU. Yeah I think so.

LUKE. Great.

RU. There'll be loads. We're so popular.

LUKE. We're not really.

RU. Luke, I know.

LUKE. Oh yeah. I hope the lads don't bring /

RU. I can't stand her.

LUKE. I did tell them not to.

 Buzzer sounds.

 Will I get that?

RU. Someone else will get it.

LUKE. It is our apartment.

RU. Yes but we invited them to our apartment.

LUKE. I don't follow.

RU. We put the heating on. The least they could do is get the door.

LUKE. I didn't put the heating on.

Silence.

Buzzer sounds again.

RU. You didn't put the heating on?

LUKE. I. Yeah, no I'll get that. You leave six seconds after me. (*With a smile.*) So people don't think I was forcing myself upon you.

RU. Like rape?

LUKE. Ru!

RU. Were you going to rape me?

LUKE. No!

RU. Luke, did you intend to rape me?

LUKE (*almost shouting*). I did not INTEND to rape you.

Silence.

RU. That didn't sound great.

LUKE. It did not.

Buzzer goes again.

Yeah, I'll get that.

RU *smiles.* LUKE *leaves.*

RU *stands, staring after him. She makes for the door but then remembers where the other thing is located. Sounds of people entering. She goes to a box near the corner of the room and takes out another thing that holds the thing that holds the dip. As she does the door flies open and in walks* VAL *wearing a tiger mask.*

Scene Three

Have You Taken Leave of Your Senses?

VAL *closes the door behind her. She looks around the room, tears her mask off, throws it and her bag on a chair. She then rips her coat off and stands in the centre of the room. She pauses before she speaks.* RU *is frozen in horror as the exact person she did not want at her party has just walked in. She does not want* VAL *to see her.*

VAL (*laughing*). Oh you are a riot, Tiernan! Such interesting and sexy facts you know about nature – Oh. Hello. I'm actually having a conversation with my new friend here. Who is he? He's new and you don't know him. What's that? Oh, you want a 'quiet word' in the box room with me? Well, I'm busy. Ah-ah, you made yourself quite clear last night. (*'Please, Val, I love you'.*) Do you? Well, I don't. I can safely say there's no love, no love of any kind, between us. It's alright, Tiernach, I have this under control. I know how to deal with. This. How dare you? You think you can just swan in to this soirée and bend down on your bent knee and offer me the moon? You have another thing coming to you, pally. Sorry, who do you think you are? I don't care if you can't breathe without me, I'm not your goddamn inhaler. No that wasn't a stab at your dust allergy. Listen, hey. Shut up. I'm not the kind of girl who responds to threats, or pleas or. Or cakes or sandwiches or whatever else you have to throw at me. In the buffet[1] of life I am not a sandwich. You are looking at su'shi[2]. Do you have any idea how difficult su'shi is to construct? Hmm? What you think you're some sort of su'shi architect? I. Am. Su'shi. Diamond su'shi. And no. You can't just pick su'shi up, bring it for a day out in the sun and leave it in a hot car with no windows rolled down. Because I'll tell you this, and I mean it, that su'shi that you loved. That su'shi will poison you. It will poison you dead. Oh stop crying, we all have tear ducts. You're making a scene. You're a stranger to me now, do you hear me, a stranger. Oh hello, stranger, lovely to meet you, I'm Val and I'm fantastic. No I don't know you. I know Tiernachnamach, my new friend, my new gentleman caller. He's been there for me through thick and thin. And they have been the most sensual seventeen minutes of my life. Get up off

1. Pronounced BuffET (hard T)
2. Pronounced SUH-SHI

your knees, you bin. It's over, do you hear me? Do you
understand now, it's over!

VAL *turns around to leave and spots* RU. RU *has been
engrossed in* VAL's *speech and lets out a shriek when* VAL
clocks her.

They both get a fright.

Ru, what are you doing? Are you following me?

RU. What? No /

VAL. Sliding into rooms after me /

RU. No I wasn't /

VAL. Staring at me, drooling, taking note of my figure /

RU. Val, I live /

VAL (*gasps*). You fancy me.

RU. No!

VAL. Then why are you in here with your pants down?

RU. They're not down.

VAL. Well, not now.

RU. Val /

VAL. Lust, Ru, gets us all in the end.

RU (*raising her voice*). Val. I live here.

VAL. There is really no need to shout.

RU. I'm sorry.

VAL. That's fine.

Pause.

RU. Okay. What are you. Doing? Here.

VAL. Have you had your hair done?

RU. What?

VAL. Your hair. You've had it done.

RU. Oh. Yeah, yes I suppose I have had it. Done.

VAL. Yes the last time I saw you it was /

RU. Up.

VAL. Red.

Look at each other suspiciously.

It's terribly nice.

RU. Oh, thank you.

VAL. Terribly nice indeed.

RU. Thank… you.

Silence.

VAL. So you and Barry, how are you and Barry.

RU. Luke.

VAL. That's what I said.

RU. You said Barry.

VAL. No I didn't.

RU. Yes. You said Barry. Do you know Barry?

VAL. You are mistaken, I said Luke. I did not say Barry. I did not say, whatever you are saying I said. You are putting words in my mouth, because Barry was not the word I used. Okay? The word I used, the person I said was Luke. I said Luke. You are going out with Luke and I said LUKE.

Door opens, LUKE *enters.*

LUKE. Ru, are you still in here – Oh shit.

VAL. Hello, Luke.

LUKE. Val's here.

RU. Val's here.

VAL. And Ru was in here. Watching me. It was weird.

LUKE. Ru, Val's here.

VAL. You might have to keep an eye on that.

RU. I can see that.

VAL. Looks like she might be a gay. For me.

LUKE. Val, yeah, yes. Val. I didn't see you come in. Did you come in with?

VAL. The lads.

LUKE. Which ones?

VAL. All of them

LUKE. Right but specifically?

VAL. Michael?

LUKE. No, sorry he's not here yet.

VAL. That's okay.

RU. Luke.

LUKE. Val.

VAL. Mmm?

LUKE. You don't have a drink. Can I get you a drink?

VAL. This is different to your last place, Luke.

LUKE. Yes. It's a different place.

VAL. Oh, is that it?

LUKE. Yes, it's not the same place.

VAL. Oh yes, that's it. I was at your last place, see.

RU. Yes. You were.

VAL. I was. I was at your last place at your last party. Do you remember? Her hair was.

RU. Up.

VAL. Red.

LUKE. Yes, we remember. (*Laughing nervously.*) You weren't a big fan of my glasses.

VAL. Your what?

RU. Luke's glasses. You broke /

VAL. Luke doesn't wear glasses.

RU. Luke's wine glasses.

VAL. Oh yes that's right. Your glasses. Your wine glasses. I had a little accident and broke one.

RU. Seven.

VAL. Pardon?

RU (*smiling*). Seven.

VAL (*laughing*). I don't think it was seven.

RU (*still smiling*). No it was. It was seven.

VAL (*laughing*). No I don't think it was seven.

RU (*still smiling*). Definitely. A set of six and a spare one.

VAL (*forcing laughter*). Well, I don't think old Ruey here has the best memory!

RU (*feigning laughter*). Well, I remember you and I remember the glasses.

VAL (*immediately halting any smile or laughter*). And I suppose you're looking for reparations, hmm? I suppose that's why you invited me to this party? To skim my wallet. I suppose that's why Ru asked for a quiet word in the box room, to corner me for money!

RU. What the fuck?

LUKE. Oh my god.

VAL. Well, let me get my goddamn cheque book out.

> VAL *picks up her bag and takes a cheque book and a pen out of it. She begins aggressively scribbling in the book.*

RU. Out. I want you out.

LUKE. Ru, get her out.

VAL. Hang on, ladies and gentlemen, wait till old Val ponies up the dough! We're down wine glasses, seven of them, seven, she says. We've been drinking our SuperValu swill from cups, mugs, leaves that we've fashioned into goblets. Sometimes our hands. We cup our goddamn hands together and sup and pray that no wine escapes. And you know why? Because Val broke all our wine glasses! Because Val destroyed all our receptacles. Because Val ruined our lives. Well, here's your blood money, Ru, here's your recompense. The bone's dry, Ru, the marrow's gone, baby.

VAL *rips a cheque off the book and hands it to* RU. RU *stands still, breathing calmly.* LUKE *is frozen on the other side of the room.*

LUKE. Baby?

RU. I won't say it again.

VAL. Well, no wait, read the cheque.

RU. I won't say it again.

VAL. No hang on you'll like this. Give it a. Read.

RU. You'll be leaving my house now.

VAL. Read the cheque, Ru.

RU. Have you taken leave of your senses, get the fuc– /

VAL (*shouting*). READ THE FUCKING CHEQUE, RU.

RU *stares at* VAL *for a moment.* VAL *smiles at her.* RU *then looks down to read the cheque.*

Out loud.

RU. 'Pay: Ru and Luke, my squishiest friends. Sum of One Hundred and Fifty Glasses Only. For services rendered. Val.' Then she's just drawn a winky face.

VAL *erupts in a fit of laughter*

VAL. Your faces. Your… (*Laughing.*) That isn't even a real cheque book.

RU: 'The Bank of Sass.'

VAL. You should have seen. Who writes cheques? (*Wiping tears from the outer corners of her eyes.*) Oh. Wow.

LUKE. That was. A good. One. Val.

VAL *stops laughing and stares at* LUKE. *All three freeze for a moment.* VAL *looks like she's ready to pounce, as does* RU. LUKE *looks like he may faint.*

VAL. I know, Luke.

RU. Drink! Drink. You have no drink. How ru-rude of us.

VAL. Well, you said it not me, Ru Rude! Is this a bedroom?

RU. Not at the moment.

VAL. Because there's no bed?

RU. Because there's no bed.

VAL. Hmm. Not what I would have done.

LUKE. Val, red or white?

VAL (*gesturing at* RU*'s hair*). I was positive it was red.

LUKE. Wine, wine the wine. Red or white wine.

VAL. Oh the wine, yes I'd like some wine.

LUKE. Okay, after you.

VAL. Ooh, here's your twin, Ru. Luke can't wait to get me all lubed up. You'd like that too wouldn't you, Ru? You could have your way with me again.

RU. There is no again, I didn't do it the first time.

VAL. Only cus I caught you. If I'd have known you were both so eager I would have worn one of my saucy nightgowns.

RU *starts. She stares at* VAL. RU *and* LUKE *stare at each other.*

What, why are you looking at each other?

LUKE. After you, Val!

VAL. Oh, he's mad for it! Follow us into the bedroom, Ru.

LUKE *shoots a terrified look at* RU*, as he leaves the room with* VAL. *As they go out* MAE *comes in, carrying her handbag.* VAL *and* MAE *stare at each other momentarily.*

Scene Four

His 25 Best Qualities

MAE. Hello.

VAL. Oh. Hello.

MAE. Do I know you?

VAL. When did you get here?

MAE. About eight. Have we met?

VAL. Never. Did you come alone?

MAE. Excuse me?

VAL. Alone, alone did you come alone?

LUKE. Wine, wine, remember wine? Okay out we go.

VAL. Lovely to see you.

> LUKE *and* VAL *leave the room.* MAE *stares after* VAL.

MAE. Who's she?

> MAE *stares after the door for a moment then sits and puts her head in her lap.*

RU (*whispering*). Baby? Nightgown? Barry. Barry.

> MAE *looks up at* RU.

MAE. What?

RU. Nothing.

MAE. What have I done, Ru? I've been a fool.

RU. I beg your pardon?

MAE. I've pushed him away. That's why he's acting so strange.

RU. But, Mae, earlier /

MAE. Earlier Mae was crazy. I've just been talking to Genevieve.

RU. Jesus. You called her? It's nine o'clock.

MAE. She doesn't mind. She made me see that I was acting insane.

RU. What did she say?

MAE. She said Mae, you're acting insane.

RU. Did she?

MAE. Yes. She's really got her head screwed on. She said I don't know how to be happy.

RU. Right.

MAE. Ru. Think about it. He has never done anything to make me distrust him.

RU. He has done, literally, loads of things.

MAE. He's a wonderful man. So many qualities. His twenty-five best qualities. One, he's genuinely funny. Two, he's intelligent. Three, he's graceful, such grace for a man, you've never seen such grace. He moves like a dream. Four, spontaneous, five, explosive, six, terrific looking /

RU. He's not terrific looking.

MAE. Seven, a tease.

RU. Can you not do the full twenty-five?

MAE. How can I not? He's perfect.

RU. Okay. Maybe. Let's talk about Barry. The first time you spent the night together, you had an epileptic fit and he went downstairs and ate ice cream until you stopped.

MAE. He thought I was having a nightmare.

RU. That's not better.

MAE. Why are you being so negative, you're usually so diplomatic. I made a mistake with the nightgown. I'm seeing things that aren't there.

RU. I'm not sure that you are. He's not. Exactly. Brilliant.

MAE. Come off it, Ru. He's perfect. I'm ruining our love, aren't I? I constantly feel like he's going to find someone better than me. I'm so anxious all the time. I need to see Genevieve. She calms me. Can I invite her here please?

RU. I would just really rather if you didn't invite your therapist to our house-warming.

MAE. It's an apartment and she's a life coach.

RU. Okay /

MAE. Ru, please. You don't understand. Just stop this has just gotten out out out of h-hand.

RU. Okay, listen calm down. Let's not call your therapist.

MAE. Life coach.

RU. Life coach.

MAE. She coaches me through life.

RU. Okay just calm down.

MAE. She's my best friend. I can't breathe, I can't /

RU. Alright okay, just. Stop. Sit down.

MAE. I can't sit down, I'll die.

RU. That's ridiculous, just /

MAE. It's not ridiculous, stop calling everything ridiculous. I'll die if I sit down.

RU. Okay, fair. What do you need?

MAE. My shoes, I I I need to take them off, my feet are swelling.

MAE *tries to kick her shoes off unsuccessfully, it turns into a stressful jig. She starts to quietly hyperventilate.*

RU. Stop okay here, I can help you.

MAE *sits in a chair while* RU *takes her shoes off.*

Better?

MAE. Yes. Can you hold them up high please?

RU. Pardon?

MAE. Elevate the shoes please, Ru, it calms me to see them up high!

RU. What?

MAE. Ru, can you hold my bloody shoes in the air please?

RU *holds a shoe in each hand high above her head.* MAE *looking at the shoes, begins to rock from side to side and rub her chest with her right hand*

RU. Here they are, look, okay?

MAE. Okay. Yes. Okay.

RU. Okay?

RU *attempts to bring the shoes down but* MAE *inhales sharply so she holds them above her head.* RU *then starts to make the shoes do a little dance. She begins to hum a tune. As* MAE *is hyperventilating, she watches the shoes dance and begins to clap along to the tune.*

MAE (*beginning to breathe normally again*). Okay.

RU. Okay they're coming down now.

MAE. Ah!

RU. Okay, okay. Slowly.

MAE. Thank you, Ru. I really need to box my own ears!

RU. Just maybe breathe?

MAE (*breathing deeply*). Is this a bedroom?

RU. No.

MAE. Because there's no bed?

RU. Not necessarily.

MAE. Because you could put a bed in here.

RU (*snapping slightly*). It's just not a bedroom.

MAE. Okay, wow.

RU. Sorry. Are you quite calm?

MAE. Yes. Forgive me. Genevieve says that panic is the enemy of the state.

RU (*pause*). She really knows her stuff that one.

MAE. She really does. I miss her.

RU. Mae, I think the best thing for you to do, right now.

MAE. Tonight?

RU. Tonight. The best thing for you to do would be to enjoy yourself.

MAE. How can I possibly?

RU. Well. Happy people are attractive. If you're smiling and thinking happy thoughts, you'll be more relaxed. And people will want to be around you.

MAE. And Barry?

RU. Sure. Barry is people so he will. Want to be around you.

MAE. So. If I pretend I'm happy. People will like me?

RU. That is what they say, isn't it.

MAE. Barry will like me?

RU (*reluctantly*). Yes.

MAE. Can you show me?

RU. Sure. Just start to smile.

MAE *tries to smile but is clearly upset*.

Well, no, not like that, that's terrifying.

MAE. Like this?

MAE *tries again*.

RU. Yeah. Sort of. Better. Now try laughing.

RU *does a laugh and* MAE *copies her. The first time* MAE *tries it sounds like she is crying.* RU *demonstrates again. They practise laughing for a bit.*

Okay I think that's enough.

MAE. Thank you, Ru. I'm sorry I'm like this.

RU. It's fine. Really it is. It's. Not your fault.

Scene Five

Dry Run

There is a knock on the door and LUKE *sticks his head in.*

LUKE. Sorry to, sorry. Ru, quick word.

RU. Of course.

MAE. Luke, of course, please come in.

LUKE. In. Without. Mae.

MAE. Oh. Oh yes. Of course. Ru. I will see you outside?

RU. I'll follow you out.

MAE. Please do. Incidentally have you seen Jessica's eyebrows? She really pushed the boat out.

MAE *leaves, with her handbag.*

LUKE. So, I think we may have something of a mess on our hands.

RU. Right.

LUKE. Val.

RU. Did you get her a drink?

LUKE. Yeah, so she /

RU. Luke, she's not well.

LUKE. Yeah I know. So.

RU. Seriously, Luke, she is fucking insane. How do you work with her?

LUKE. Well.

RU. Didn't you tell me she tried to take legal action against someone in work she thought called her a prostitute.

LUKE. Yes but /

RU. But then it turned out that she had just overheard a conversation where a man was telling his colleague about his prostate /

LUKE. Ru!

RU. / cancer.

LUKE. Ru.

RU. Sorry.

LUKE. Val is in the bathroom.

RU. And?

LUKE. Val has locked herself in our bathroom.

RU. Oh.

LUKE. With a bottle of gin.

RU. The gin? How did she find the gin? We didn't put the gin out.

LUKE. I hid it under the sink. She found it when she was rummaging.

RU. Why were you letting her rummage?

LUKE. I got distracted. When I looked around she was under the sink. She said she was looking for something to wash off the stench of mediocrity from this party

RU. Right.

LUKE. Then she found the gin.

RU. Okay.

LUKE. Anyway she's locked herself in the bathroom. She seems to be muttering to herself and /

RU. Seems to be?

LUKE. Well, no, she definitely is muttering to herself. And periodically screaming 'Give him up, he's mine.'

RU. Really? And people. Can people hear her?

LUKE. People can definitely hear her. There's no doubt in. Not a. Shadow. More than that, people. Would like to use the bathroom.

RU. Yes. Of course.

LUKE. Should I do. Something?

Pause.

RU. No.

LUKE. That's probably the last thing I thought you would say.

RU. Luke. She's been with Barry.

LUKE. Who? Val?

RU. Yes Val. It's Barry.

LUKE. Bollox.

RU. She is. She has been. With. Barry. Mae thinks Barry has been, is being with someone else. She found a nightgown.

LUKE. You said that was for his mother.

RU. Yes but then Val mentioned that she had a nightgown. And that it was saucy.

LUKE. Ah, come on. What does that even mean?

RU. She asked about Barry. She asked how Barry and I were. I told her I was with Luke and she said that's what I said and I said no you said Barry and then she lost her mind trying to correct me.

LUKE. She mentioned Barry's name and she has a nightgown.

RU. A saucy nightgown.

LUKE. A saucy nightgown. That's your evidence?

RU. Yes. (*Pause.*) And and then she said baby.

LUKE. Baby?

RU. Barry always says baby, Mae says it now. And Val does too.

LUKE. Okay just breathe, sweet. Potato. Face.

RU. Luke, eat something!

LUKE. Yeah okay.

RU. Luke, he is the worst kind of person.

LUKE. He is. He really is but let's just /

RU. No! Oh, Barry, I'm Barry I try to sleep with everything. Barry. We've all slept with Barry. Oh, we've all slept with

Barry. Well, I haven't slept with Barry because he's a prick. But Barry's tried. Luke, he's done this to Mae so. Many. Times.

LUKE. Okay, alright. That's enough. Okay. I think we should stop talking about Barry. He's not even here. Let's just get Val out of the bathroom and keep Mae away from the balcony.

RU. I hate him, Luke.

LUKE. I know.

BARRY *sticks his head around the door.*

BARRY. Who do you hate?

LUKE. Barry.

RU. Barry.

BARRY (*joyfully*). Barry!

LUKE. Hi. Barry.

BARRY. Hello, ladies and gents, happy house-warming I brought you a special spoon.

BARRY *hands* RU *a large ladle with tags on it. It is wrapped in several brightly coloured ribbons that only cover a portion of it.*

LUKE. Thanks, Barry. Ru loves soup.

RU. No I don't.

LUKE. What are you doing? Have you been inside?

BARRY. No not yet. I met Jessica across the road, she was going to the bathroom in Finnegan's. Said yours was ocupado. Hey, what's wrong with her face?

RU. Nothing.

LUKE. Ru, would you like a drink? You haven't had a chance to. Sit down. And. Drink.

RU. Actually, Luke, I would like a word with Ba– /

LUKE. No why don't you go on out and get a drink and chat with Mae. We'll be out right after you.

BARRY. Mae's here already?

RU. Yes.

BARRY. Fine.

LUKE. Great.

BARRY. Good.

> *Pause.*

RU. I'll go grab a drink and Mae and trot right back in here,
shall I?

LUKE. No.

BARRY. What?

LUKE. No.

BARRY. Why?

RU. Why not? How was your emergency, Barry?

BARRY. It was. Emergent.

LUKE (*quietly*). Nope.

RU. I hope it was important.

BARRY. It was. It really was.

LUKE. Ru.

RU. Luke, can I speak to you outside for a second please?

> *Pause.*

LUKE. Yeah. Sure.

> RU *leaves and* LUKE *slowly follows her.* BARRY *stares at
> the door for a moment. He then moves towards the mirror.*

BARRY. Hey, I'm Barry. Barry yeah. I'm Barry. Bar. Bar Bar.
Like the elephant, exactly. So where are you from? Kewl
kewl, I don't where that is – (*Laughs.*) Yeah I'm from
Dalkey, my mum is a solicitor. No. Yeah no. Actually. I'm
a solicitor. A big one. A big solicitor. I'm the biggest
solicitor. If you, pick up what I am putting down...

> LUKE *comes back in the room quickly, still holding the
> spoon.*

Scene Six

She's Here

BARRY. So.

LUKE. Hi.

BARRY. Nicely done.

LUKE. Yeah.

BARRY. Not really, though. That was very clumsy.

LUKE. Yeah.

Pause. LUKE does not make eye contact with BARRY.

BARRY. What's wrong?

LUKE. Ru knows.

Pause.

BARRY. She what?

LUKE. She knows.

Pause. Next lines spoken simultaneously.

BARRY. How the fuck did she find out? What did you say to her, are you out of your head, why hasn't she tried to murder me yet? Is she going to tell about us? Because according to you, it was nothing. Nothing.

LUKE. Not about that, about you and your. What the fuck do you think I'd tell her that for, it wasn't even, nothing it was nothing. I'm not out of my mind. It wasn't even anything. It was nothing.

Pause.

BARRY. What?

LUKE. What?

BARRY. What does she know?

LUKE. About Val. You fuck.

BARRY. Oh, Jesus. Val? You nearly. I mean. Christ. Wow. Crisis averted.

BARRY *holds up his hand in a celebratory fashion,
imploring* LUKE *for a high-five or a fist pump or something
of that manner.* LUKE *does not respond.*

LUKE. My girlfriend knows you're… (*Gesturing.*) with a
mental person behind her best friend's back. How is that.
Crisis averted?

BARRY. Yes but. From where I was standing. I thought your
girlfriend knew /

LUKE. No she doesn't.

BARRY. Great. We can keep pretending it never happened.

LUKE. I'm not pretending, I just don't want to talk about.

BARRY. Fine, yeah, great, grand. How does Ru know about Val?

LUKE. She doesn't, well. She put it together. Have you gotten
rid of Val? How did it go?

BARRY. Yeah not bad. She put it together?

LUKE. What do you mean 'not bad'?

BARRY. Well.

LUKE. Yes?

BARRY. Yeah. Well. It went fine for me. She was driving,
dropping me home. I asked her to pull into a garage. Told her
I needed some. Pop. Asked did she want anything. No. Asked
could I have her car keys for the loyalty card. Yeah. Took the
car keys. Locked the car from the outside. Then I shouted.
'It's over. You're mental. I hate you.' Threw the keys as far
away as I could. Then ran all the way home.

LUKE. Right.

BARRY. Mmm. So from my perspective. Not bad.

LUKE. Bit of exercise.

BARRY. Exactly, yeah. So, sorry, how does Ru know about Val?

LUKE. She doesn't know, she pieced it together. But her
evidence is bullshit.

BARRY. Oh yeah? What does she have?

LUKE. Well, Mae thinks you're… (*Gesturing.*)

BARRY. Doing sex on /

LUKE. Barry, please. She thinks you're having. Intercourse. With someone. Else. And she told Ru.

BARRY. Does she actually?

LUKE. Yes.

BARRY. I can't believe she'd think that.

LUKE. You have been with someone else. Did you not think she'd eventually realise?

BARRY. She's never copped before. She's smart as anything but not too bright if you know what I mean.

LUKE. No. I don't know what you mean.

BARRY. Well, she's not supposed to know.

LUKE. I wish I didn't know. I hate knowing. I can't lie. Don't ever tell me again. Or just break up with Mae.

BARRY. How does Mae know?

LUKE. She said something about a nightgown.

BARRY. That fucking nightgown.

LUKE. Was it for your mother?

BARRY. No.

LUKE. It was for Val?

BARRY (*nodding*). The psychotic.

LUKE. Go way.

BARRY. Yeah. She fucking loves nightgowns.

LUKE. Jesus, fair play to Ru.

BARRY. Did she guess that?

LUKE. Yeah.

BARRY. Jesus, yeah, fair play to her.

LUKE. It was the nightgown, the fact that you used to work with Val and something about the way you say baby the whole time.

BARRY. I never say baby.

LUKE. You do.

BARRY. I do not.

LUKE. Ah, you do.

BARRY. Nope. Bullshit evidence.

LUKE. Oh, utter shite. She's right, though.

BARRY. She is that.

LUKE. Listen, I've to go deal with that, em. Bathroom situation. Can you. Stay here?

BARRY. Right. Wow. Okay.

LUKE. Yeah. Do you mind?

BARRY. Well, I'd prefer not to.

LUKE. I know I know, I just need you to stay here and. Unwrap this spoon.

LUKE proffers the spoon to BARRY.

Pause.

BARRY. Now?

BARRY takes the spoon.

LUKE. Yep, Ru will want to use it almost immediately.

BARRY. She really does like soup, huh?

LUKE. She really does.

BARRY. Amazing gift, Barry.

LUKE. Exactly. So if you could just do that, I'll be back in a second and we can go get a drink.

BARRY. Okay.

LUKE goes to leave again.

Luke?

LUKE. Yeah?

BARRY. Would Ru tell Mae? About Val?

LUKE. No. I don't think so. She wouldn't want to upset Mae.

BARRY. No. Yeah.

LUKE *goes to leave.*

I will. Make a clean breast of it.

LUKE. You should. I just hope Ru doesn't run into Val again, otherwise Mae might finish you tonight.

BARRY (*laughing*). Yeah.

LUKE *leaves.*

Wait what.

BARRY *stands still thinking for a moment then begins removing the ribbons and/or cellotape from the spoon. The door silently opens and* VAL *slinks in in a cow mask. She shuts the door and* BARRY *realises he is not alone in the room. He looks up, but not at* VAL.

(*Whispering.*) Oh god.

VAL *reopens the door behind her and acts like she just came in the room.* BARRY *spins around.*

(*Laughing at the door.*) Oh that's so funny. Back in a tick, Tiernanch. (*She closes the door behind her.*) Oh. Hello. I was actually having a conversation with my new 'friends' here. Who are him? He's new /

BARRY. What are you doing here?

VAL. I was invited.

BARRY. Val /

VAL. AH. So you haven't forgotten me? Can't get me over, off your mind. Can't get my name off your lip hmm?

BARRY. Yeah. Heeey, Val. Are you. How are. You look. Did you get home okay last night?

VAL. I got home fine yes thank you. A man found, fetched my keys. I didn't even ask him to.

BARRY. That is super.

VAL. So I see you're lurking in the box room, obviously to catch me for a quiet word. Typical. Well, I'm busy.

BARRY. I honestly didn't know you were here.

VAL *looks at* BARRY *for a moment.*

VAL. That was some fun last night, wasn't it?

BARRY. Eh, well, it was. A different sort of /

VAL. Of?

BARRY. Game?

VAL. Game?

BARRY. Look, Val, I think I might pop off.

VAL. Please. Do you think I'm simple? You don't want to. Pop off. You think you can just swan in to this soirée and bend down on your bent knee and offer me some moon? You have another thing coming to you, Sally. Who do you think you are? Some kind of super star?

BARRY. What?

VAL. What do you think?

BARRY. Val. I think we should. Not communicate. Ever. Never.

VAL. What?

BARRY. I. Would just like it if we were not in contact.

VAL. And I will not respond to threats or pleas or sandwiches. I. Like. Su'shi.

BARRY. I'm sorry?

VAL. I put diamonds in my su'shi. That is me.

BARRY. Yeah, Val, I think I might leave you to it..

BARRY *makes for the door.*

VAL (*raising her voice*). You lied to me.

BARRY *stops moving.*

You lied to me. You lied to me, so many times. You said you were finished at Mae. Lie. You said you were allergic to dust. False, lie. Never even saw an inhaler. You said you wanted to get pop. LIE. You said that you love me. Lie. Why do you lie all the time?

BARRY. I'm sorry.

VAL. No. No, no sorry. Why? Why? It's not me. I'm. Really lovely. It must be you.

BARRY. I don't know.

VAL. Does it make you feel good?

BARRY. Yes.

VAL. Well, it makes everyone else feel like dirt.

Pause.

BARRY. I don't know what to say.

VAL. Don't say anything.

Pause.

Don't say anything. It will do no good. You cannot win me back.

BARRY. Well, I don't actually /

VAL. You will never win me over again. I don't care how much you love me.

BARRY. Oh. How awful. What a punishment.

VAL. Or maybe I could just tell Mae everything? It would be the perfect reason to eject you from her house.

BARRY. Well, no, don't. Do that. It's hard enough losing you.

VAL. Well, maybe I won't have to tell Mae. I could just show her the pictures I have of your genitals on my hand-held telephone with a camera.

BARRY. Look, Val, please don't. I'm talking to her tomorrow, we'll be finished. I promise.

VAL. Tomorrow? She's here now! I'll get her. Mae!

LUKE *sticks his head in the door.*

LUKE. Hey, we're all clear – no we're not.

VAL. Hi, Luke. Where's Mae?

LUKE. Mae? Mae is actually gone.

VAL. No she's not.

LUKE. She is.

BARRY. Is she?

LUKE. Yes. Ru and Mae went to buy more gin. We ran out.

VAL. No problems. I'll wait outside for them. With. My. Phone.

VAL *leaves.*

Scene Seven

Semantics

LUKE. I'm sorry, Barry, I thought she was.

BARRY. So. She's here.

LUKE. Yeah. She's here.

BARRY. She's here.

LUKE. Yeah.

BARRY. She's here. Why is she here?

LUKE. I /

BARRY. Where's Mae?

LUKE. They actually have gone to buy more gin. I asked Ru to take Mae.

BARRY. How long do we have?

LUKE. Like five minutes?

BARRY. I told you.

LUKE. I know. You told me. I know you told me /

BARRY. Well, I told you I never wanted to see her again.

LUKE. I know. I didn't invite her. I don't know why she's here.

BARRY (*getting irritated*). Yeah but she is here.

LUKE. I know she's here. I didn't invite her.

Pause.

And why should I have to keep her away?

BARRY. Jesus, don't.

LUKE. No, why am I trying to keep your side pieces /

BARRY. Side pieces, for fuck's sake, cop on will you, we're not Americans.

LUKE. Why am I preventing your women from coming to my house, where my girlfriend /

BARRY. Luke, it's an apartment.

LUKE. My home, where my girlfriend /

BARRY (*sneering*). Your girlfriend.

LUKE. Yes. My, my girlfriend. Yeah, she is mine.

BARRY. Yeah but come on, bit hypocritical, Luke /

LUKE. Look. I tried to stop her. I couldn't stop her. The lads brought her. She's here.

BARRY. Yeah she is here. And now I have to leave with my girlfriend because Val is a liability.

LUKE. She wouldn't have been as much of a liability if you hadn't /

BARRY. Ah, she would.

LUKE. And is Mae still your girlfriend? Because you told me you moved out. Is she your fucking girlfriend still?

BARRY. Look. This has all gotten. A bit. What do you care who I'm with? I mean we're not /

LUKE. I don't care. No we're not. Anything. We're not anything.

BARRY. Are we not?

LUKE. Look, it was one. I was in a bad place.

BARRY. It was last week.

LUKE. It was just one.

BARRY. It was one what?

Pause.

LUKE. Slip.

BARRY. You're right, we're not anything. So why are you getting upset when all my chickens come home goosed?

LUKE. What?

BARRY. What?

LUKE. Come home what?

BARRY. Goosed.

LUKE. That's not it.

BARRY. What?

LUKE. That's not the phrase.

BARRY. Yes it is.

LUKE. When all your chickens come home goosed?

BARRY. Yeah.

LUKE. What like. Locked chickens?

BARRY. Yeah.

LUKE (*smiling*). That's not the phrase.

BARRY. No, listen. Semantics.

LUKE. You don't know what semantics means.

BARRY. I don't see how that's relevant.

Pause.

We have fun.

LUKE. Shut the fuck up.

BARRY. What's this? Why are you so upset?

LUKE. I'm not.

BARRY. You are. Why do you care?

LUKE (*quietly*). I don't care.

BARRY. You don't care? Because you look like you care. (*Pause.*) You look like you fucking care.

LUKE (*getting louder*). No I don't fucking. Look. I tried to. I told them not to bring her. I'm sorry she's here. I. I don't even know what you were doing with her, she's fucking mental.

BARRY. I know she's mental, she's fucking crazy but she's kinda sexy and I can't. Help. It. I mean, she wanted me.

LUKE. Oh for /

BARRY. Stop now, she went for me. She stood in front of me in the elevator, when it was just the two of us and put her arse on my.

LUKE. Don't.

BARRY. I mean. What could I do? I was solid as a rock.

LUKE. Don't.

BARRY. Before I knew what was happening the lad was out and I was absolutely drilling into her arse /

LUKE. Ah, Barry, I asked you not to.

BARRY. What was I supposed to do?

LUKE. What were you supposed to do? Tell her to stop? Tell her you live with your girlfriend. Don't take your penis out. There. There's at least three things you could have done.

BARRY. Why does it matter to you? You would have done it too.

LUKE. That is bollox. I wouldn't do that /

BARRY *coming in on top of* LUKE (*verbally*).

BARRY (*mockingly*). You wouldn't do that /

LUKE. No. I wouldn't do what you did. Do you not feel guilty?

Pause.

BARRY. No.

LUKE. That's impossible.

BARRY. I don't.

LUKE. I don't believe that because I can't fucking sleep.

Pause.

BARRY. Sorry.

LUKE. What is wrong with you?

BARRY. I don't know.

LUKE. Do you not feel anything?

BARRY. No.

LUKE. Nothing?

BARRY. I don't feel anything.

Pause. LUKE *stares at* BARRY. BARRY *moves close to* LUKE.

I kissed a stranger on the dance floor of a bar while Mae was getting us drinks. I had sex with someone in her house while she was upstairs in bed. I'm in here with you. And. Nothing.

LUKE. I can't get it out of my head.

BARRY *kisses* LUKE. *The door opens silently.* LUKE *pushes* BARRY *away.* VAL *is standing in the doorway. They hear her.*

VAL. Fuck. Off.

Scene Eight

Theatrics

BARRY. Val.

LUKE. Fuck.

VAL. Fuck Val is right /

LUKE. I thought you /

VAL. What the fuck is this, boys?

> *Silence.*

> What the fuck is this?

LUKE. It's.

BARRY. We're.

LUKE. It's.

BARRY. Practice.

> *Silence.*

VAL. Practice?

LUKE. Yep.

BARRY. Mmhmm.

LUKE. Rehearsals.

VAL. Is it?

LUKE. It is.

BARRY. Yes. Just practising.

LUKE. Rehearsing.

BARRY. Rehearsing.

VAL. For?

> LUKE *and* BARRY *make a 'thinking' noise and look at each other.*

LUKE. A play?

VAL. A play?

BARRY. No /

LUKE. No listen /

BARRY. No it is /

LUKE. We joined an am-dram society for a little bit of confidence and /

BARRY. And we were cast in a famous play.

LUKE. A very famous play.

   Pause.

VAL. What's it called, quickly.

BARRY. Ahhhh /

LUKE. Ehh /

BARRY. Hot? Hot /

LUKE. Chair.

BARRY (*under his breath*). For fuck's sake.

   Pause.

VAL. Hot Hot Chair?

LUKE. Just Hot Chair.

BARRY (*under his breath*). That's not better.

VAL. I can hear you.

LUKE. It's a new play.

VAL. The very famous, new play, Hot Chair?.

BARRY. That's the one.

LUKE. Yep.

   Pause.

VAL. Okay. Do a bit.

BARRY. From?

VAL. The play. Do a bit from the play.

BARRY. It's really not ready.

LUKE. We haven't warmed up.

VAL. Okay.

VAL moves towards the door. The boys jump.

BARRY. No! No. Luke? Start the play.

LUKE. Okay fine, fine. (*Clears his throat.*) What are you doing, Mordecai?

BARRY. Jesus. I'm. Harvesting the chairs.

LUKE. Taking them in from the sun?

BARRY. That's right. The townspeople will never want to buy. Hot chairs.

LUKE. Skip to the end.

BARRY. When the farm was gone. Tiernach and Mordecai realised they were /

LUKE. Best friends. And so they sealed their friendship with a kiss.

BARRY and LUKE lean in and do a fake kiss.

BARRY. And in that moment they knew. They were all hot chairs.

Pause. They look at VAL.

Pause.

LUKE. Val, please /

VAL. Is this the face of a fool?

BARRY. No.

LUKE. God no.

VAL. No it is not.

BARRY. Val /

VAL. Quelle surprise, Barry, but you, Luke. This is quite the quelle surprise.

LUKE. What?

VAL. I expected this from him. He's a monster. I thought you were nice.

LUKE. Val. You're imagining things. This isn't at all what you think.

BARRY. It really was practice.

VAL. Shut up, Barry. When did it first happen, Luke? Recently? Barry loves theatrics. Had you signed the lease yet? You are something. Ru is going to be devastated.

LUKE. Val, please please don't say anything. This was nothing.

VAL. Oh, I have to say something, Luke, she's my best friend. Did you really think I was going to keep this from her? How could I look her in the eye knowing what I now know?

LUKE. Your best friend?

BARRY. Easy, Luke. Val, I really need to talk to you alone.

VAL. No.

BARRY. Val, please (*Pause*.) I miss you.

VAL. The last time you saw me you said you didn't think we should communicate, ever never.

BARRY. Yes I know but the time apart made me realise… I need to speak with you alone. Maybe outside this apartment? Far away.

VAL. No. I don't want to be alone with you, Barry. Not with all this information I just gleaned. All this explosive information. I'm going outside this instant to tell a stranger what you've been doing so you two don't try to murder me.

LUKE. We're not going to murder you, Val, just hang /

VAL. Just hang on a second till we murder you, I know your game.

BARRY. Val, I actually definitely still love you.

VAL. Come off it, Barry, I've seen the movies.

LUKE. Val, please god don't tell anyone. It was a mistake.

BARRY. I think we could still be together.

VAL. No, Barry, see that would never work because I wouldn't pay your rent.

Buzzer sounds.

Oh that must be the girls, let's go do this in front of everyone, shall we?

VAL *flings open the door and turns left. The boys look at each other then follow her, leaving the door open.*

Scene Nine

She Could Be a Prostitute

A few moments later RU *and* MAE *walk past the door, coming from the right with a bottle of gin and an open bottle of wine.* RU *sees the door open and walks in the room.* MAE *follows her closing the door behind them.* MAE *is still carrying her handbag.*

MAE. About thirty-three million.

RU. Fuck off. How did you work that out?

MAE. Apparently on average, people spend nought-point-four-five per cent of their lives doing intercourse. So if there's seven-point-four thousand million people on earth, multiply by point-nought-nought-four-five, that's about thirty-three million.

RU. Are having sex right now?

MAE. Yes. Well. That figure includes children.

RU. Oh.

MAE. I'd need to know the statistic of people the legal age.

RU. How did you do that so quickly?

MAE. It's really simple maths, Ru.

RU. Is it?

MAE. Genevieve is wonderful at maths.

RU. Jesus.

MAE. She just understands me.

RU. Yeah well, I mean, you pay her.

MAE. Don't make it sound so dirty. She's not a prostitute.

RU. No sorry I wasn't implying that at all /

MAE. Don't get me wrong she could be.

RU. What?

MAE. Genevieve. She could be a prostitute.

RU. Could she?

MAE. Of the highest class, because she's very beautiful.

RU. Oh. Yeah.

MAE. I don't even think you could call her a prostitute, she's far too classy.

RU. Mmm.

MAE. No one would be able to afford her!

RU. She'd be very expensive?

MAE. I could probably afford her.

   Pause.

RU. How often do you see Genevieve?

MAE. Oh sort of once every, forty-two hours.

RU. That is a lot of life-coaching sessions.

MAE. Yes well, I need a lot of life coaching.

RU. Do you? Are they all in her office?

MAE. No, gosh no, lives aren't spent in offices, Ru. That's what Genevieve says.

RU. You work in an office.

MAE. Yes but life.

RU. You practically live in your office.

MAE. Yes but I have a life, Ru.

RU. So where do you meet Genevieve?

MAE. She has a darling little cottage by the canal, we go there most evenings.

RU. And what do you do in your sessions?

MAE. Mainly laugh.

RU. And?

MAE. Oh how we laugh.

RU. What else, though?

MAE. Well, Genevieve has cleverly themed our sessions. We have cheese session, wine session, cheese and wine session and also hug therapy.

RU. I have so many questions but I'll just start with, hug therapy?

MAE. Oh it's incredible, we lie on her couch and just hold each other for hours.

RU. Right.

MAE. Mmm.

RU. Mae, would it be so bad. If Barry were to. Not be around any more.

MAE. Oh. But I love Barry.

RU. Why?

MAE. Well. You don't know what he's like when we're alone.

RU. What does Genevieve think of Barry?

MAE. She says I have to come to that decision on my own. She doesn't want me to resent her. Which is mental because she's literally perfect.

RU. Mae. Does Barry make you feel as good as, say, Genevieve does?

MAE. No one makes me feel as good as Genevieve does, Ru, but you can't be in love with your life coach!

RU. Can you not?

The door flies open and in walks VAL *followed by* LUKE.

VAL. Ladies!

RU. Val.

MAE. Hello.

LUKE. Ru, don't /

VAL. Now, Luke. Don't spoil the surprise!

MAE. What's your name?

VAL. I'm Val, I'm /

LUKE. A prostitute.

RU. Luke?

VAL. I'm Val and I'm not a prostitute, even though I could be.

As VAL *is introducing herself to* MAE, BARRY *comes into the room.*

BARRY. Luke, where the fuck did she. Heeeeeeeey. Girls.

LUKE. Everyone's here, Barry.

RU. Barry.

MAE. Barry!

VAL. Prick.

BARRY. Barry.

RU. Well, I wasn't going to. But since we have a bit of privacy.
    Mae. Barry has something to tell you.

BARRY. No I don't.

RU. Barry.

BARRY. No, Ru.

RU. Fine. Coward. I'll do it.

VAL. I'll take it from here, Ru.

RU. What?

LUKE. Val. Ru was speaking. Please don't /

RU. Don't what?

VAL *takes* MAE *by the hand.*

VAL. Mae, I think we could be friends. Really good friends. Even better friends than Ru and I.

MAE. That's nice.

RU. We're not friends.

VAL. Ru, please I'm speaking. But, Mae, I have to tell you something about Barry. This isn't going to be easy to hear but just know that you have the most wonderful hair that I have ever seen.

RU. Okay, no, Mae /

VAL. Fine, Ru, I was trying to deliver the bad news with some finesse but here, I'll just throw it at her like a raw steak. Mae, Barry has been sleeping with Luke.

Silence.

RU. You are unbelievable, that's ridiculous.

Silence.

Luke? Isn't she unbelievable?

VAL. I saw them kissing in here. Tonight.

MAE. You were with Luke?

RU. No he wasn't.

MAE. Were you?

RU. Luke?

BARRY. We were locked, Mae, it was only once.

MAE. Once? Luke?

VAL. Twice, they kissed tonight.

LUKE. And Val, Barry was with Val for ages.

MAE. Luke?

VAL. Don't be so dramatic, Luke, it was twenty-seven weeks. Max. And I don't even like him, Mae.

Silence.

MAE. Of course you were.

BARRY. Mae /

MAE. No. Don't.

BARRY. I know.

MAE. No really. This time. Just don't.

BARRY. Okay.

MAE. Did you think I wouldn't find out?

BARRY. I don't know what I thought. I'm sorry for hurting /

MAE. Barry, do you have any idea /

BARRY. I know /

MAE. No you don't. I stood up for you.

BARRY. But I don't deserve it.

MAE. I know that. I don't know why I did it.

Pause.

BARRY. You're not really in love with me, Mae. You just. Think you should be.

MAE. Please don't give me advice, Barry. I have Genevieve for that.

BARRY. Yeah I know.

MAE. Your things will be in the garden tomorrow. Don't contact me again.

BARRY. Jesus, Mae, let's not lose our heads here, I can stay until next week, can't I?

MAE. No you cannot. I need to see Genevieve.

BARRY. Mae /

MAE. Barry, just leave it. I'm sorry, Ru, I have to go.

VAL. Mae, perhaps I can accompany you outside and we could grab a drink? And then we can continue this friendship the way we've always wanted to.

MAE. I can't remember your name.

VAL. Excellent. Gentlemen. Ru.

MAE *leaves the room and* VAL *trots out after her.*

BARRY. Fuck.

LUKE. Ru?

Silence.

Ru?

Silence.

Ru, please say something.

RU. You wanted to move in.

LUKE. Ru, I'm so sorry.

RU. You wanted to move in. You asked me. You let me sign the lease. You signed the lease. Why did you sign the lease?

LUKE. I didn't know, I /

RU. Why did you sign the lease?

LUKE. I wanted to live with you.

RU. Then why did you fuck Barry?

LUKE. I don't. Know.

RU. So you did.

LUKE. I don't /

RU. Are you gay?

LUKE. No I'm not. I was. Sc– drunk and. I don't know. I've never felt like that before. I don't feel like that now.

RU. But you were just going to carry on hanging out with him?

LUKE. I didn't know what to do, he's the only one I could talk to.

RU. Is he?

Silence.

LUKE. I didn't mean that.

RU. Get out.

LUKE. Ru, please.

RU. Luke, get out.

LUKE. Ru, please. Don't make. Let's talk. I haven't been talking to you, I swear I can explain.

RU. Get the fuck out, Luke. I don't want to look at you.

Pause.

Close the door.

LUKE *leaves and closes the door after him.*

Silence.

BARRY *looks around the room. He makes a loud noise as if to say 'glad that's all over'.*

BARRY. Ahhhh. That was. Weird.

RU *is fixed on the door/wall. Staring anywhere except at* BARRY.

You alright, Ru?

RU *still fixed.*

Silence

I think I'll just /

RU. Fuck off, Barry.

RU *leaves.*

End of play.

A Nick Hern Book

Sauce and *All honey* first published as a paperback original in Great Britain in 2022 by Nick Hern Books Limited, The Glasshouse, 49a Goldhawk Road, London W12 8QP

Designed and typeset by Nick Hern Books, London
Printed in Great Britain by Mimeo Ltd, Huntingdon, Cambridgeshire PE29 6XX

A CIP catalogue record for this book is available from the British Library

ISBN   978 1 84842 955 0

www.nickhernbooks.co.uk

facebook.com/nickhernbooks

twitter.com/nickhernbooks